What Went Wrong
with
Vatican II

A Forthright Edition™

Sophia Institute Press awards the privileged title "A Forthright Edition" to a select few of our books that address contemporary Catholic issues with clarity, cogency, and force, and that are also destined to become classics for all times.

Forthright Editions are *direct*, explaining their principles briefly, simply, and clearly to Catholics in the pews, on whom the future of the Church depends. The time for ambiguity or confusion is past.

Forthright Editions are *contemporary*, born of our own time and circumstances and intended to become significant voices in current debates, voices that serious Catholics cannot ignore, regardless of their prior views.

Forthright Editions are *classical*, addressing themes and enunciating principles that are valid for all ages and cultures. Readers will turn to them time and again for guidance in other days and different circumstances.

Forthright Editions are *charitable*, entering contemporary debates solely in order to clarify basic issues and to demonstrate how those issues can be resolved in a way that strengthens souls and the Church.

Please feel free to suggest topics and authors for future Forthright Editions. And please pray that Forthright Editions may help to resolve the crisis of the Church in our day.

What Went Wrong with Vatican II

The Catholic Crisis Explained

by

Ralph M. McInerny

A
Forthright
Edition™

from

SOPHIA INSTITUTE PRESS®
Manchester, New Hampshire

Sophia Institute Press®

Box 5284, Manchester, NH 03108

1-800-888-9344

www.sophiainstitute.com

Library of Congress Cataloging-in-Publication Data

McInerny, Ralph M.
    What went wrong with Vatican II : the Catholic crisis
    explained / Ralph M. McInerny.
        p.   cm.
    Includes bibliographical references.
        ISBN 0-918477-79-4 (pbk. : alk. paper)
        1. Vatican Council (2nd : 1962-1965) I. Title.
BX830 1962.M39   1998
262'.52 — dc21   98-29115 CIP

98 99 00 01 02 10 9 8 7 6 5 4 3 2

Contents

What Went Wrong
with
Vatican II

Introduction

"Bliss was it in that dawn to be alive, but to be young was very Heaven."[1] Thus wrote William Wordsworth in a bout of enthusiasm for the French Revolution, perhaps possible only because he had the English Channel as a buffer between himself and it. Many felt the same exhilaration during the halcyon days of the Second Vatican Council, whose sessions were held from 1962 to 1965.

A new day had dawned. Windows were to be thrown open and the fresh air of modernity let in. This was indeed the day the Lord had made.[2]

Surprise had been expressed when John XXIII announced that there would be a council. The usual conditions for calling such a high-level meeting of the bishops

of the Church did not seem present, and, as if taking this
into account, the Holy Father stressed that this would be
a *pastoral* council, not one called to deal with doctrinal
matters. Church teachings, the implication was, were
about as clear as they could be. What was wanted was a
renewed effort on the part of Catholics to evangelize the
world, an updating, an *aggiornamento*.

∞

JFK and John XXIII: They Weren't What They Seemed
John XXIII reminded many of Friar Tuck, who had been
chaplain to a band of benevolent thieves. He seemed
everyone's grandfather, someone who, understanding
all, would forgive all. He was often linked with John F.
Kennedy, who had been elected president of the United
States in 1960 and in one stroke had given Catholicism
a social acceptability it had never had before in this
country. The two Johns would somehow make the Faith
palatable to the modern world. How could anyone fail to
respond to the genial, pudgy little Pope? And how could
anyone resist the charm of JFK, a celebrity, a star, who
brought near frenzy to otherwise sober folk?

President Kennedy's posthumous reputation, unfortunately, sinks lower every day. If he made it seem almost

chic to be Catholic, it is difficult to grasp what, if anything, he himself really believed.

On the other hand, anyone who takes the trouble to
discover what kind of man John XXIII really was will find
it difficult to recognize the media persona with which he
was invested. It is forgotten now that early in his papacy
he issued a directive requiring Latin to be fully restored
as the language of instruction in seminaries and pontifical institutions. His sense of the dignity and authority of
the papal office is clear from the encyclical he wrote on
Pope Leo I.[3]

The real John XXIII does not look like the patron of
our modern decentralized Church, whose Liturgy is celebrated in more languages than were known at Babel. And
Vatican II, like the French Revolution, receives for the
most part mixed reviews. "Liberty, Equality, and Frater-
nity"[4] sounded wonderful, but a lot of heads would roll.
So, too, *aggiornamento* had its attractions, but did so
many cherished traditions have to go?

∝

The Strength of the Church in the 1950s
What did the preconciliar Church look like? It would be
very wrong to imagine that it was something broken and

in need of repair. Here are some impressions of the Church in the United States just before the bishops convened at the Vatican to begin the council.

In his monumental 1979 book, *The Battle for the American Church*, Msgr. George Kelly provided a little *tour de monde*, listing dozens of Catholic intellectuals here and abroad who had world-class standings as artists, writers, and thinkers. "The English Catholic firmament," he noted, "was studded with stars,"[5] as was the Continent.[6] The United States had its Catholic intellectual luminaries as well.[7]

Still, there was in the postwar world a sense that Catholics had not yet come into their own insofar as the intellectual and cultural life of the nation was concerned. In many ways, this mirrored the self-criticism of the WASP elite when it looked toward England during the nineteenth century. This discontent among Catholics had a galvanizing effect on Catholic colleges and universities, initiating a drive toward excellence that was soon to have astonishing results, both good and bad.

Msgr. Kelly's evocation of the preconciliar scene compares interestingly with that of the acerbic English Catholic Evelyn Waugh. Like many British writers, Waugh tended to be condescending toward the former colonies. In his book *The Loved One*, he made the burial customs of California a metaphor for the nation. It would be easy to document his credentials as an anti-American. But Waugh was also a Catholic, a convert, and one whose loyalty to his adopted Church was profound.

In 1949, he wrote for *Life* magazine an article called "The American Epoch in the Catholic Church." It is a remarkably positive and optimistic piece. In it, Waugh says that American Catholics are the richest and liveliest body in the universal Church. He is impressed by American Catholic achievements in education, in thriving parishes, and in ambitious building programs. Moreover, he admires the spiritual revival exemplified by Thomas Merton and the spread of contemplative monasteries across the land. Waugh had two chief impressions: first, that there is as great a variety in the outward forms of Catholicism in America as can be found in Europe, and second, that Catholicism "is not something alien and opposed to the American spirit, but an essential part of it."[8]

Waugh ends his piece with a virtual identification of Catholicism and the American way of life: "There is a purely American 'way of life' led by every good American

Christian that is point-for-point opposed to the publicized and largely fictitious 'way of life' dreaded in Europe and Asia. And that, by the Grace of God, is the 'way of life' that will prevail."[9] Waugh's title conveys his ultimate judgment. He foresees an American epoch in the Catholic Church.

This positive attitude is matched by Jacques Maritain in his 1958 book *Reflections on America* and was, in a way, anticipated by Alexis de Tocqueville, who, in *Democracy in America*, prophesied that Americans would stream into the Catholic Church.[10] Not unlike John Henry Newman, he felt that the final sorting out would involve only two groups: those who relinquish Christianity and those returning to the Church of Rome.

Waugh's 1949 article sketches what, for many Catholics, must seem like a long-lost Golden Age for the Catholic Church in America. Msgr. Kelly's book confirms such a view. For example, here are some statistics that Msgr. Kelly gleans from the Catholic Directory. In 1950:

- There were 60,000 priests in the United States, with some 25,000 more men in seminaries preparing for ordination.

• There were 150,000 religious teachers in the schools.

• There were five million children in Catholic schools, from kindergarten to college, and five million more in non-Catholic schools receiving religious instruction.

The practice of the Faith? Seventy-five percent of married Catholics attended Mass every Sunday. Fifty percent received Holy Communion at least once a month. Eighty-five percent of single people went to Mass every Sunday, and fifty percent of them received Holy Communion at least monthly. College-educated Catholics were the most faithful of all.[11]

Msgr. Kelly draws a number of conclusions from such statistics. For the majority of Catholics, the Church was still the vehicle whereby they became assimilated to American society and moved upward on the social and economic scales. The faithful were loyal to their pastors and their bishops and to the teachers they had in the Catholic school system. Catholic parishes were centers of social life, sometimes ethnic, but more usually little melting pots of their own. A Catholic elite was emerging from the Catholic educational system, and lay apostolic movements for social justice, international peace, family life, and spiritual perfection flourished.[12] Who can blame Msgr. Kelly for taking pride in that picture?

∽

The Decline of the Church After the Council

Then came Vatican II, calling for renewal, for new and more effective ways to disseminate the truth, and for greater attention to the training and preparation of priests. Religious life must be renewed; all members of the Church should grow holy. *Gaudium et Spes*, the longest document of Vatican II, even laid out a comprehensive and stirring vision of the role the Church should play in the modern world.

Catholics expected a quantum leap forward and assumed that, in the United States, in particular, a bright picture would be made even brighter. That did not happen. Something very much like the opposite happened.

"The spirit of Vatican II" swept Latin from the altar and from the psalter as well. Now a little more than thirty years after the council's close, the majority of priests are probably incapable of saying Mass in Latin. The Liturgy has been altered and altered again. Priests face the people as presiders, and the watchword is lay participation. And, while there certainly are more lay people milling around in the sanctuary, the pews are not as full as they were: Mass attendance has plummeted.

It is estimated that in the wake of the council, ten million Catholics stopped attending Mass regularly, a decline of thirty percent. It is estimated that in some major cities, only thirty percent of Catholics now attend Sunday Mass. The decline has been particularly severe among the young, even those educated in the Catholic system. There has been a precipitous decline in enrollment in the Catholic schools. Fewer babies are baptized.[13]

Comparing the preconciliar Church and the aspirations of Vatican II with events of the past thirty years forces us to ask: What went wrong? Can anyone pretend that things have improved? There are some bright spots, but it is undeniable that the faith of Catholics has been shaken and that our way of living no longer distinguishes us from other Americans. Astonishingly, this decline in the Church has come about under the banner of Vatican II. And sometimes it seems as if we are being told that this bad news is good news if only we can understand the spirit of the Second Vatican Council.

As we near the third millennium of the Christian era, it seems an apt time to reflect on Vatican II. It is the central event of Church history in our time. Clearly it was a providential occurrence. Its sixteen documents, although with varying force, are the measure of the Faith of Roman Catholics. Properly understood, it was a great blessing for the Church — properly understood.

That is our task here, and a formidable one it is indeed.

∞

The Authority of Vatican II

Since the close of the council, tens of thousands of pages have been written discussing the meaning and proper implementation of hundreds of points made in its sixteen documents. In some of these many books are heard the voices of critics who claim that the Second Vatican Council contradicts earlier councils and other solemn teachings of the Church, and therefore is itself invalid.

To these critics I say that whatever problems may be posed by the documents of Vatican II, contradiction of earlier councils cannot be one of them. It is the Pope who calls an ecumenical council into session; he monitors the work of the assembled bishops; and he promulgates the documents expressing the judgment of the bishops. When he does that, those documents become the measure of our Faith.

That which makes Vatican II valid is what made Vatican I, the Council of Trent, and every other council valid. To accept one council is to accept them all; to reject one council is to reject them all: we cannot have pick-and-choose conciliarism.

I do not, therefore, defend the Second Vatican Council against those who think it is suspect and in contradiction to earlier councils or to solemnly defined teachings of the Church.

On the contrary, I take as a necessary premise the fact that we are bound by the teachings of the Second Vatican Council. Yes, I grant that many passages in the sixteen documents of Vatican II require careful study and interpretation, but study that begins with an animus against the council is bound to go astray. For my part, I embrace the council wholeheartedly and with gratitude. My aim is to clear away the impediments to its proper fulfillment.

And that itself is urgent work. For among those who accept the authority of the council, some have tried to use its documents to justify practices that the council Fathers never foresaw or intended. A comprehensive evaluation of such abuses of the council documents is essential for understanding much of the history of the Church since Vatican II. It would produce a very interesting judgment on the kaleidoscope of changes in the Church these last thirty years, changes that many have welcomed and that many abhor.

Nonetheless, although I accept the council and reject the abuses of it, I have not in these pages attempted such a kaleidoscopic survey. Volumes could be devoted to it, but I believe they would obscure rather than illuminate the most fundamental answer to the question, "What went wrong with Vatican II?"

To give the very deepest answer to that key question, I have written a lean and focused book. I purposely avoid hundreds of important but lesser issues that might be raised by a thoughtful and receptive reading of the documents of Vatican II.

Why? So that I can concentrate on the one issue that gives life to so many of the other controversies swirling around the council and the Church today: the crisis of authority, which is the single most important force stirring up the choppy seas through which the Barque of Peter has been navigating since the close of Vatican II.

For thirty years, the Catholic faithful have been confused and troubled by a single question: Where does authority in the Church really reside? Only a sure answer to this question will expose the roots of the problem of what went wrong with Vatican II. Only a sure answer to this question will enable us to see what must be done to bring the council back to its intended goals.

☙

Did Vatican II Presage the End Times?

As we approach the end of the second millennium, many imagine that time itself is coming to an end. In serious Catholic circles, this fear is often fueled by the large number of recent apocalyptic warnings reported in real or alleged appearances of the Blessed Virgin Mary. Many believe that in 1917 her apparition at Fatima, Portugal, foretold the end of the world; but a stronger case can be made that Fatima predicted the very real, although unintended, effects of Vatican II.

Jacinta, one of the three children to whom Mary appeared at Fatima, once said, "I can't say how, but I saw the Holy Father in a very large house, kneeling before a table with his face in his hands. He was crying. Many people were in front of the house; some were throwing stones, while others were cursing him and using foul language."[14]

Has anyone described better the beleaguered state of the Papacy and the Magisterium of the Church since Vatican II?

Some have even concluded that the Church simply went off the rails in the early 1960s and that we are now living in the end times. War seems to have broken out within the Church Herself: appealing to Vatican II, prominent theologians deny the authority of the Pope and urge the faithful simply to ignore it. Yet how can the council be right and the Pope be wrong?

At the same time, many conservative Catholics have denounced the council itself as a doctrinal aberration, arguing that its teachings are in conflict with traditional Catholic doctrine. Yet, to appeal from the present Pope to earlier popes, from one ecumenical council to earlier ecumenical councils, creates insuperable difficulties. If the Church was not protected from error in Vatican II, why should one imagine that earlier councils are more reliable?

Yet, if the council is not flawed, what is flawed?

What went wrong with Vatican II? Massive defections of priests and religious may not have been the aim of the council, but they came about in great numbers. The impudent attitude of prominent theologians toward the Magisterium and their dismissal of the Holy Father, whether Paul VI or John Paul II, may not have been intended by Vatican II, but their dissent is an all too familiar feature in the Church today. Displays of weakness by pastors and bishops may not have been intended by the council, but how many priests and bishops explain and defend the Faith with the courage and faith of the Holy Father?

Indeed, why does the Pope stand alone, patiently and forcefully addressing the evils of our day, bringing the Faith to bear on the world in which we live?

To answer these questions, and to discover the remedy for the sorrowful decline of our Church in recent decades, we must consider the council itself, and key events that occurred in its aftermath.

Fatima's ringing call for prayer and penance suggests that the fault may lie not only in our bishops or theologians, but in ourselves. It may be that the renewal John

XXIII hoped the council would effect will only finally be experienced by following the message of Our Lady of Fatima. The crisis of authority that plagues the postconciliar Church may be a punishment for our own sins, and for the sins of others in the Church.

Chapter One

The Forgotten Teachings
of the Council

On October 11, 1962, Pope John XXIII opened the Second Vatican Council in St. Peter's Basilica with a speech full of hope and promise. Recalling the Church's previous councils, the Pope said that Vatican II was called to reaffirm the teaching role of the Church in the world.

In calling this vast assembly of bishops, the latest and humble successor to the Prince of the Apostles who is addressing you intends to assert once again the Church's Magisterium [teaching authority], which is unfailing and perdures until the end of time, in order that this Magisterium, taking into account the errors, the requirements, and the opportunities of our time, might be presented in exceptional form to all men throughout the world.[15]

The problem facing us, the Pope pointed out, is the same today as it has ever been: Men stand either with the Church or against Her; and rejection results in bitterness, confusion, and war. Councils testify to the union of Christ and His Church and promulgate a universal truth to guide individuals in their domestic and social lives.

Far from being motivated by foreboding and concern for the modern world, Pope John XXIII was full of optimism. Many had come to him lamenting the state of the world, seeing it in steep decline. We live, they implied, in the worst of times. Not so, said John XXIII:

> We feel we must disagree with those prophets
> of gloom, who are always forecasting disaster,
> as though the end of the world was at hand.
>
> In the present order of things, Divine Providence is leading us to a new order of human relations which, by men's own efforts and even beyond their very expectations, are directed toward the fulfillment of God's superior and inscrutable designs.[16]

John XXIII discerned even in troubling modern circumstances possibilities for the Church to fulfill Her mission of preaching the gospel of Christ more effectively.
Throughout this opening address, he was filled with
exuberant optimism.

And he was quite clear about what he wanted the
council to accomplish: the defense and advancement
of truth.

> The greatest concern of the ecumenical coun-
> cil is this: that the sacred deposit of Christian
> doctrine should be guarded and taught more
> efficaciously.[17]

John XXIII said that in our day there is already
sufficient clarity about the teaching of the Faith. The
emphasis of the council should thus not be doctrinal but
pastoral. It should consider how best to convey the truth
of Christ to the modern world.

He said that errors are best dealt with in a gentler
way than heretofore. The same charity should suffuse our
dealing with our "separated brethren." Here the Pope
strikes the note that will fuel the ecumenical movement
among the churches.

The closing prayers of his address convey the simplicity and faith of John XXIII:

Almighty God! In Thee we place all our confidence, not trusting in our own strength. Look down benignly upon these pastors of Thy Church. May the light of Thy supernal grace aid us in taking decisions and in making laws. Graciously hear the prayers which we pour forth to Thee in unanimity of faith, of voice, and of mind.

∞

O Mary, Help of Christians, Help of Bishops, of whose love we have recently had particular proof in thy temple of Loreto, where we venerated the mystery of the Incarnation, dispose all things for a happy and propitious outcome and, with thy spouse, St. Joseph, the holy Apostles Peter and Paul, St. John the Baptist, and St. John the Evangelist, intercede for us to God.

∞

To Jesus Christ, our most amiable Redeemer, immortal King of peoples and of times, be love, power, and glory forever and ever. Amen.[18]

❦

Lively Debate Characterized the Sessions

The Second Vatican Council met in four sessions. The first session opened, with the papal address just recalled, on October 11, 1962, and closed on December 8 of the same year. Pope John XXIII, whose idea the council was, died on June 3, 1963. He had expressed the hope that, if he were not still alive when the council ended, he would watch its joyful conclusion from Heaven.

His successor, Paul VI, called for the second session to begin on September 29, 1963, and it ran until December 4, 1963. The third session was held from September 14 to November 21, 1964. The fourth and final session ran from September 14 to December 8, 1965.

Anyone reading the exchanges between the bishops during the sessions of the council must be impressed by the high level of the discussion. For example, the discussion of the Declaration on Religious Liberty was feared by some to fly in the face of earlier Church teaching, obviously a serious reason for caution. Proponents, respecting this concern, were eager to allay it. Participants in the debate opposed one another against a background of a shared concern for the tradition of the Church. Some would reduce this spirited and often profound exchange to a conflict between liberals and conservatives, but such a reduction misses the depth of the discussion.

Some interventions in the council are more impressive than others, of course, but what is lacking from these actual sessions is the kind of ideological dogfight reported at the time in periodicals and shortly thereafter in the multi-volume histories of the council.

Reading some of those accounts of the council sessions, especially those written at the time, is not an edifying experience. Even so relatively sober a book as Fr. Ralph Wiltgen's *The Rhine Flows into the Tiber* portrays the debates as no nobler than a playground quarrel. Perhaps the saddest description is Fr. Wiltgen's account of Alfredo Cardinal Ottaviani being silenced:

> On October 30, the day after his seventy-second birthday, Cardinal Ottaviani addressed the council to protest against the drastic changes which were being suggested in the Mass. "Are we seeking to stir up wonder, or perhaps scandal, among the Christian people, by introducing changes in so venerable a rite, that has been approved for so

many centuries and is now so familiar? The rite
of Holy Mass should not be treated as if it were a
piece of cloth to be refashioned according to the
whim of each generation." Speaking without a
text, because of his partial blindness, he exceeded
the ten-minute time limit which all had been re-
quested to observe. Cardinal Tisserant, Dean of
the Council Presidents, showed his watch to Cardinal Alfrink, who was presiding that morning.
When Cardinal Ottaviani reached fifteen minutes,
Cardinal Alfrink rang the warning bell. But the
speaker was so engrossed in his topic that he did
not notice the bell, or purposely ignored it. At
a signal from Cardinal Alfrink, a technician
switched off the microphone. After confirming
the fact by tapping the instrument, Cardinal
Ottaviani stumbled back to his seat in humiliation.
The most powerful cardinal in the Roman Curia
had been silenced, and the Council Fathers
clapped with glee.[19]

Looking back on it from a distance of thirty-five years,
a reader is more likely to be astonished by the reported

reaction of the council Fathers than he is likely to share in it. Fr. Wiltgen was writing in 1977, and his account of the sessions was generally praised for its objectivity, but he, too, operates with the simplistic notions of conservative and liberal.

Such accounts as Fr. Wiltgen's — and let me stress that his is as evenhanded as one is likely to find — seek and find a drama in the proceedings that doubtless characterized the politics outside the hall. There are good guys and bad guys, and in the end the good guys win.

But it is not in histories of the council, contemporary or otherwise, that the council itself should be sought. Nor are the records of the discussions between the bishops the final word. Where, then, is the council itself to be found?

❧

Catholics Cannot Reject the Council

Sixteen official council documents emerged from sessions in which schemata were proposed, altered, replaced, argued, and ultimately voted on. Each of the conciliar documents can be parsed back into a written record of such debates and discussion, but there is no need to characterize such debates in terms of obscurantists and enlightened progressives — not even when, as in the case of the Declaration on Religious Liberty, the debate defines itself in terms of such opponents. For in the end, it is the final document that trumps all earlier arguments and discussion. Once voted on and promulgated by the Pope, a conciliar document is no longer the victory of one side or the triumph of a faction: it becomes part of the Magisterium of the Church.

There is little doubt that, in the minds of many observers, reporters, and even *periti*, a struggle was going on between the traditionalists and the innovators. Even if this mirrored a struggle among the Fathers of the council, when the dust settled, when the final vote was taken, when a document was approved and promulgated by the Pope, it was the product of the teaching Church. And in Her role as teacher, the Church is guided by the Holy Spirit. Whatever spirited battles took place in the course of the council, the only spirit that matters is the Holy Spirit, whose influence on the promulgated document is guaranteed.

Studying the record of discussions among the bishops, of drafts of documents, and the proposals for change can, of course, aid us in understanding the final approved results. But it is the final documents as approved by the bishops and promulgated by the Pope that contain the official teaching of the Catholic Church. And Catholics have a duty to accept the teaching of a council.

The *Catechism of the Catholic Church* spells out the infallibility of an ecumenical council:

> "The Roman Pontiff, head of the college of bishops, enjoys this infallibility in virtue of his office, when, as supreme pastor and teacher of the faithful — who confirms his brethren in the Faith — he proclaims by a definitive act a doctrine pertaining to Faith or morals. . . . The infallibility promised to the Church is also present in the body of bishops when, together with Peter's successor, they exercise the supreme Magisterium," above all in an ecumenical council.[20]

Consequently, the teachings of the Second Vatican Council are the official teachings of the Church. That is why the more than thirty years that have passed since the close of the council are evaluated by the Church in the light of the council.

That is why Paul VI and John Paul II have regarded their papacies as dedicated to the implementation of what was decided during those fateful three years of the council.

That is why rejecting the council is simply not an option for Catholics.

And that is why Archbishop Marcel Lefebvre's schismatic movement involved an internal incoherence. He sought to appeal to earlier councils in order to discredit Vatican II. But that which guarantees the truth of the teaching of one council guarantees the truth of them all. Popes Paul VI and John Paul II exhibited a long patience with Archbishop Lefebvre. Eventually, he undertook to consecrate new bishops in defiance of the Vatican, and no more patience was possible. He was excommunicated.[21]

✁

What Vatican II Says About the Pope

The same long patience has been shown to dissenting theologians who have undertaken to appoint themselves the final arbiters of Catholic truth and to inform the faithful that they need not accept the teachings of the Holy Father.

Often, they justify this dissent by citing "the spirit of Vatican II," which one theologian explains as follows:

> Vatican Council II was an example of democracy in action. Opinion had been widespread that, with the definition of papal infallibility, councils would no longer be needed or held. After Vatican I, it seemed the Pope would function as the Church's sole teacher. Vatican II, however, showed what could be accomplished in the Church when all the bishops worked together. There was significant input from theologians (some formerly silenced). Protestant observers made an important contribution.[22]

The spirit of Vatican II urges us to balance what the Magisterium says with other points of view throughout the Church. Magisterial teaching is referred to as the "official" teaching of the Church, as if there were another, rival teaching that could trump the Pope.

But what does Vatican II itself say about this? After speaking of the college of bishops and the collegiality that characterizes the episcopal office, Vatican II declares that not even bishops, acting apart from the Pope, have any authority in the Church:

The college or body of bishops has for all that no
authority unless united with the Roman Pontiff,
Peter's successor, as its head, whose primatial authority, let it be added, over all, whether pastors
or faithful, remains in its integrity. For the Roman
Pontiff, by reason of his office as the Vicar of
Christ, namely, and as pastor of the entire Church,
has full, supreme, and universal power over the
whole Church, a power which he can always
exercise unhindered.[23]

Obviously, if even bishops, singly or collectively, have
no authority apart from the Pope, no other group in the
Church has such authority. No other group has the role
of accepting or rejecting papal teaching and advising the
faithful that they may rightly reject papal teaching.

In a word, according to Vatican II, the Pope is "the
supreme pastor and teacher of all the faithful,"[24] the successor of St. Peter, the Vicar of Christ on earth. He is
head of the college of bishops. He can himself, independent of the bishops, exercise the supreme Magisterium.

In light of this, there seems simply to be no way to
read the teachings of Vatican II and find in them any

basis for the postconciliar view promoted by some theologians that papal teaching can be legitimately rejected by Catholics.

Yet some theologians continue trying. They suggest that Catholics are bound only by Church teaching that is infallible by dint of being formally and solemnly defined. According to them, such instruments of the Magisterium as encyclicals should be treated with respect, but Catholics have the option of setting their teaching aside.

∾

Catholics Must Submit to the Pope

Is there any support in Vatican II for such a conception? Is acceptance on the part of the faithful limited to solemnly defined teachings, clearly infallible for that reason? The Second Vatican Council also answers this question clearly and forcefully:

> This loyal submission of the will and intellect must be given in a special way to the authentic teaching authority of the Roman Pontiff, even when he does not speak *ex cathedra*, in such wise, indeed, that his supreme teaching authority be acknowledged with respect, and that one sincerely adhere

to the decisions made by him, conformably with his manifest mind and intention, which is made known principally either by the character of the documents in question, or by the frequency with which a certain doctrine is proposed, or by the manner in which the doctrine is formulated.[25]

Unfortunately, some theologians, particularly moral theologians, for reasons we will examine in subsequent chapters, have simply rejected this clear teaching of Vatican II. They have come to see their role as one of criticizing, passing judgment on, and even dismissing magisterial teaching.

There is no surer protection against this attempted usurpation than the documents of Vatican II themselves and particularly the passages just quoted from the Dogmatic Constitution on the Church, *Lumen Gentium*.[26]

There is, of course, something odd in the effort to quarrel with what are obviously teachings of the Church and therefore require religious assent from Catholics. It is almost as if the aim were to discover how little one need believe. But surely, as Vatican II urges, it should be the mark of Catholics that they take on the mind and heart of the Church and show gratitude for God's great gift of the Magisterium.

The calibration of Church teachings that is suggested by distinguishing between the ordinary and extraordinary Magisterium is an important one, but it does not justify any distinction between magisterial, papal teachings that need to be accepted by Catholics and those that do not.

Indeed, to advise Catholics to ignore clear magisterial teachings is to advise them to reject the clear teaching of Vatican II. How ironic that the council should be invoked as warrant for dissenting from the Magisterium when it is precisely the council that rules this out.

To accept Vatican II is to accept what the council says about the Magisterium and the Catholic's obligation to obey it.

As we will soon see, public and sustained rejection of the Magisterium and of this clear teaching of Vatican II — largely by dissenting theologians — has caused and sustained the crisis in the Church.

Chapter Two

1968: The Year
the Church Fell Apart

On July 25, 1968, in the encyclical *Humanae Vitae* ("Of Human Life"), Pope Paul VI reaffirmed the Catholic Church's condemnation of artificial contraception. The news was received as a surprise — indeed as a bombshell. Already in the first reports there was the added shock that Catholic theologians in large numbers were publicly rejecting the papal encyclical. After what would soon seem to have been a three-year lull, all hell was breaking out in the Catholic Church.

John XXIII had removed the topic of contraception from the agenda of the Second Vatican Council. Instead, he appointed a commission to guide him in the matter, reserving to himself the final decision. There were at the time claims that many new factors — medical, biological, psychological, sociological, and demographical — cast doubt on the traditional prohibition. Obviously the council could have gotten bogged down sifting through such claims and opinions. The Pope relieved them of the burden.

John XXIII died in the course of the council, and Paul VI was elected Pope. On the matter of contraception, he both retained and enlarged the commission appointed by his predecessor. Of course, this left the impression that the Church was reconsidering Her prohibition of artificial contraception. Presumably a reconsideration could go in either of two directions: the ban might be continued or it might be lifted. With that alternative in the air, months passed. The council ended in 1965, and still there was no decision. Years passed — almost three more years.

∞

Humanae Vitae *Angers Many Catholics*
During this time there was not merely silent expectation. Those who thought that a lifting of the ban was possible and desirable aired their views. Rumors circulated that the commission was advising the Pope that the old

arguments against artificial contraception no longer worked. It became received opinion among theologians that artificial contraception would no longer be prohibited by the Magisterium of the Church.

It is important to understand the atmosphere of those days. Moral theologians of repute, on and off the papal commission, were writing in favor of lifting the ban on artificial contraception. This became, of course, a matter of classroom discussion in Roman Catholic colleges, in seminaries, and beyond. The discussion spilled over into publications of wide circulation. Pastoral care was affected by the expectation that soon the Church would rescind Her prohibition. Couples preparing for marriage could hardly be expected to be guided by a prohibition whose days were numbered. No doubt, confessors, too, dealt differently with penitents who were using contraception.

That is the background against which the announcement in July of 1968 came as a veritable bombshell. An angry reaction was inevitable on the part of those who had tied their professional reputations to the removal of the prohibition. Those who had taken part in the work of the papal commission, who had urged, as they thought persuasively, the case for lifting the ban, felt betrayed. How dare the Pope ignore their advice?

What exactly did Pope Paul VI say? His judgment was contained in an encyclical that, like the conciliar documents, is often referred to but seldom read. Those who, within hours of the announcement of the issuance of the encyclical, signed an advertisement in the *New York Times*, banding with other moral theologians in rejecting the papal teaching, could not have read the encyclical. They knew its import, the one and central thing: Paul VI had left the prohibition in place.

℁

Priests and Laymen Denounce the Encyclical

Some events in those first days after the announcement of the encyclical now have an almost comical character. In Adelaide, Australia, a strange scene played itself out at St. Francis Xavier Catholic Cathedral. When worshipers emerged from Mass on August 4, 1968, they were met by students carrying signs of protest and passing out pro-contraceptive pamphlets. A small booth had been set up bearing the legend "Catholic Contraceptive Center." An irate man rushed to the booth and hurled it over. It was set up once more and again was overturned.

The following Sunday, in Santiago, Chile, a group of eight priests and one hundred and fifty laymen, having concealed themselves in the cathedral overnight, refused to admit those who came for Sunday Mass. The group held the cathedral for fourteen hours, during which time the priests among them celebrated Mass. They explained that they were protesting the wasteful spending in preparation for Pope Paul VI's impending visit to Bogotá, Columbia.[27]

A Swiss moral theologian, Fr. Anton Meinrad Meier, resigned from his post at Solothurn seminary in protest against *Humanae Vitae*. Fr. Meier said that the encyclical "subordinates common sense to biological laws and the Magisterium of the Church and therefore contradicts itself."[28]

Msgr. Joseph Gallagher, passing through Rome on his return from a pilgrimage to the Holy Land, paused to issue a statement announcing that he was dropping the title of monsignor. Fr. Gallagher, a translator into English of the acts of the Second Vatican Council and a former professor of Thomistic philosophy at St. Mary's Seminary in Baltimore, explained his move by saying that the title of monsignor should imply a special allegiance to the Holy Father. *Humanae Vitae* made it impossible for him to continue to extend such fealty. In his global view, Fr. Gallagher found *Humanae Vitae* "tragic and disastrous."[29] While Paul had preserved the inner logic of papal authority, he had gravely wounded its rational acceptability, or so Fr. Gallagher thought. The priest found the teaching of the new encyclical intellectually, emotionally, and spiritually repugnant. His statement went on to liken acceptance of the encyclical's judgment to accepting the right of the Inquisition to employ physical torture.[30]

Meanwhile, back in Baltimore, Lawrence Cardinal Shehan, Fr. Gallagher's bishop, expressed regret and advised his priest to read once more the council documents that Fr. Gallagher himself had translated.[31]

The Catholic press in Britain spoke out on the encyclical. *The Tablet*, the senior Catholic weekly, highly respected in England and elsewhere, was sharply critical. Its comments addressed the status of the encyclical rather than its contents. "This will raise, inevitably, questions as to the status of encyclicals, their authority and binding force. Whether they will be devalued or endorsed we cannot predict. A new chapter in the relationship of the Pope with his bishops and with the faithful at large has

now opened on a somber note." The paper foresaw doubt
and dismay among some Catholics, a new bravado among
others, and mutual distrust.[32]

Fr. Hans Küng, professor of theology at Tübingen, said
on Zurich radio that Catholics should take *Humanae
Vitae* seriously and read it loyally, but if they concluded
that marital happiness would be jeopardized by following
its principles, they should follow their own consciences.
In doing this, they should not think of themselves as sin-
ners. All in all, he thought *Humanae Vitae* represented a
crisis, the most serious of modern times. He saw a silver
lining, however, in that he felt it would force the Church
to reevaluate Her concepts of authority and infallibility.
"This must be done in recognition of the fact that the
Divine Spirit time and again renews the Church despite
all the errors of popes, bishops, theologians, priests, and
men and women."[33]

It was the rare bishop who spoke negatively about
the encyclical. To prove the rule, however, there was,
of course, that hierarchical free variable Archbishop
Thomas Roberts, a retired Jesuit missionary, who had
in the past spoken favorably of birth control. He saw
a gloomy future. The encyclical, he thought, would

intensify the Church's crisis of authority, confuse Catholics, and bring about defections among priests already worried about birth-control problems. As for the faithful, the retired Bishop of Bombay said that they had already been making their own decisions about contraception and would continue to do so.[34] Archbishop Roberts's reaction was predictable by anyone who had read his book *Contraception and Holiness*.[35]

∞

The Encyclical's Source Is Disputed

This reaction to *Humanae Vitae* created an incredible situation. The Pope, as Vicar of Christ and successor to St. Peter, had merely reaffirmed and explained the Church's long-standing ban on artificial contraception, yet dissenters were accusing him of creating disruption in the Church.

He was described by friends as calm and relieved after his long ordeal. Behind him lay the reports of commissions, letters from bishops, appeals by Nobel Prize winners, pleas of the faithful, and literally years of personal study. Calm and relieved he may have been, but one must also imagine him braced for a further storm. The possibility of that storm, even its inevitability, must have been clear to him while he pondered his decision. As was now evident, the prospect of continued controversy had not affected the anguished conclusion to which he had come.

Only a future historian would be able to record in detail the steps that had gone into the writing of Paul VI's encyclical *Humanae Vitae*. For the moment, however, in the popular mind, there were at least two versions of what had gone on.

In one, the Supreme Pontiff of the Roman Catholic Church, impressed by majority reports of papal commissions, and swayed by the advice of some bishops and cardinals, was moving toward a historic reversal of the Church's position on birth control when he was brought to heel by conservatives in the Vatican. Paul VI, in this version, was a prisoner of the old guard, the remnants of the papal bureaucracy that had survived the reforming spirit of the recent ecumenical council. Now the Pope was sealed away in medieval indifference to the actual world, and neither his presence at Castel Gandolfo nor his impending visit to South America could hide the fact that he was a prisoner in the Vatican. By insisting on the authority of the papacy, he had brought it into disrepute, even perhaps put it on the road to decline and fall.

There is a second version, the one suggested by Msgr. Ferdinando Lambruschini, professor of theology at Lateran University in Rome, when he presented the encyclical to the press on the morning of July 29, 1968. The Pope, Lambruschini said, had acted with great courage.[36] Despite tremendous pressure, despite the possibility of open defiance, of disaffection, even of schism, he had maintained the Church's traditional position on the nature of marriage, the position reiterated by the recent ecumenical council. The Pope had taken his stand; he could do no other.

No matter which version one accepts, the Pope had spoken, and the position of the Roman Catholic Church on artificial contraception was once again clear and unequivocal.

Or was it? The Pope had indeed spoken, but what precisely was the force of his letter?

∞

Theologians Challenge the Encyclical's Authority
Msgr. Lambruschini, a member of the commission the Pope had appointed, seemed to go out of his way to

insist that the teaching of *Humanae Vitae* was "not irreformable."[37] He pointed out that the encyclical was not to be considered an infallible pronouncement; nonetheless, it was an authentic pronouncement of the teaching authority of the Church, and Catholics must give it "full and loyal assent."[38] Yet, according to Lambruschini, the encyclical did not close theological discussion of the subject of birth control, although "it does not leave the question of the regulation of birth in a state of vague uncertainty."[39]

Obviously Lambruschini was speaking of theological subtleties that only professionals could be expected to grasp. *Humanae Vitae* maintained that artificial contraception is against God's law because it was contrary to the nature of marriage and conjugal love. In a word, it claimed that contraception is a violation of the natural law. In that case, how could the judgment be considered reformable?

∞

Confusion Grows Among the Laity

In the days that followed, perplexed Catholics would wonder how something that was now morally wrong might in the future be said to be morally right.

Surely contraception did not fall into the same class as the older prohibition of eating meat on Fridays. Everyone knew that while the obligation to do penance was incumbent on every Catholic, abstinence from meat on a particular day of the week was merely a Church law that could be — and had been — abrogated. Would a future generation of Catholics be told by the Church that artificial contraception is licit?

In any case, on the practical level, should there ever have been any doubt among Catholics as to where their Church stood on the matter of artificial contraception? Wasn't Pope Paul VI simply reaffirming the traditional position by deciding that there were no good reasons to change that position?

In fact, it was just on the level of practice that the difficulty resided.

Few of the Catholic laity had personally studied the reasoning behind the Church's prohibition of artificial birth control. In the past, whether or not they always abided by it, they had accepted the ban as one of the elements of their belief, one more mark that set them off from so many of their fellows. In the years prior to *Humanae Vitae*, however, many Catholics had heard other voices in the Church that carried quite a different message. The ban was said to be a matter for doubt and discussion. Catholics heard that it would come under review at the Second Vatican Council. Special commissions had been appointed by the Pope. The Pope himself would soon announce a change.

Meanwhile, many Catholic couples were told by their confessors that they could licitly, in good conscience, in anticipation of the change, employ contraceptive devices. These confessors were acting on the opinions of theologians (not every confessor is a theologian, nor vice versa). However nuanced the discussion among theologians might have been, the advice that filtered down to married couples prior to *Humanae Vitae* was that they could make up their own minds on the matter in anticipation of the coming decision. It is hardly surprising that many began to use contraceptive devices, usually the pill.

It is important to grasp what was involved here if one wants to see the dilemma facing Catholic couples. Prior to the appearance of *Humanae Vitae*, new advice had been substituted for older advice; and the new advice was accepted in pretty much the same manner as the old.

The priest had said that such-and-such was the Catholic position, and Catholics simply accepted it. Theologians used to assure them that birth control was a mortal sin; now, prior to *Humanae Vitae*, theologians in increasing numbers told them it was not, that it was a matter for individual decision. This judgment was passed on to the faithful in confessionals, in newspapers, and in conversation, and the practice of a great many Catholics underwent a dramatic change.

With the appearance of *Humanae Vitae*, these married couples were put in the difficult position of hearing that the advice they had been given was wrong. They could not continue to use the pill or any other contraceptive device. And priests must instruct their parishioners accordingly. Said Msgr. Lambruschini at the Vatican press conference on July 29: "All those who have in recent years incautiously taught that it is lawful to use artificial contraceptive practices to regulate births and have acted accordingly in their pastoral guidance and in the ministry of the confessional must change their attitude."[40] The target of this remark was not merely a random priest here or there. The Archdiocese of Munich had, some time before, issued official instructions to priests that a Catholic

54

couple who, "under their mutual Christian responsibility, seeking the true welfare of the child, come to believe that they cannot avoid a contraceptive conduct, must not be rashly accused of abusing marriage."[41] Now even Cardinal Doepfner, Archbishop of Munich, was in a rather difficult position.

Chapter Three

Whose Church
Is It, Anyway?

It is doubtful that Catholic couples who had been using the pill were concerned, that July morning in 1968, about the plight of cardinals such as Doepfner. Rather, they were most likely questioning whether they had been misled by their priests into a marital practice they must now abandon. The temptation of such couples to rebel against the Church can be understood, yet it was quickly overshadowed by a public rebellion by the clergy.

Throughout July 29, the very day Pope Paul VI's encyclical was made public, it became clear that *Humanae Vitae* was encountering massive clerical resistance. It was being treated with scorn and contempt everywhere. Long before they could have read the encyclical, Catholic theologians, sociologists, and journalists were dissociating themselves from its reported teaching. Said Fr. Robert Johann, S.J., to the *New York Times*, "The hope, I think, is that educated Catholics will ignore this document."[42]

Fr. Charles Curran, associate professor of theology at the Catholic University of America and vice president of the American Theological Society, spearheaded an effort to solicit signatures for a statement to be published about the encyclical. When the statement was first issued, there were eighty-seven signatures. The number of those wishing to associate themselves with Fr. Curran's refusal to accept *Humanae Vitae* was to swell in subsequent days to more than two hundred.

Published in the *New York Times* on July 30, 1968, above the signatures of over two hundred theologians, the Curran statement is a critical document for anyone hoping to discover what went wrong with Vatican II:

As Roman Catholic theologians, we respectfully acknowledge a distinct role of hierarchical Magisterium [teaching role] in the Church of Christ. At the same time, Christian Tradition assigns theologians the special responsibility of

evaluating and interpreting pronouncements of
the Magisterium in the light of the total theological data operative in each question or statement.
We offer these initial comments on Pope Paul VI's
encyclical on the regulation of birth.

The encyclical is not an infallible teaching.
History shows that a number of statements of
similar or even greater authoritative weight have
subsequently been proven inadequate or even
erroneous. Past authoritative statements on religious liberty, interest-taking, the right to silence,
and the ends of marriage have all been corrected
at a later date.

Many positive values concerning marriage are
expressed in Paul VI's encyclical. However, we
take exception to the ecclesiology implied and the
methodology used by Paul VI in the writing and
promulgation of the document. They are incompatible with the Church's authentic self-awareness
as expressed in and suggested by the acts of the
Second Vatican Council itself.

The encyclical consistently assumes that
the Church is identical with the hierarchical

office. No real importance is afforded the witness of the life of the Church in its totality; the
special witness of many Catholic couples is
neglected.

It fails to acknowledge the witness of the separated Christian churches and the ecclesial commu-
nities; it is insensitive to the witness of many men
of good will; it pays insufficient attention to the
ethical import of modern science.

Furthermore, the encyclical betrays a narrow
and positivistic notion of papal authority, as illus-
trated by the rejection of the majority view presented by the commission established to consider
the question, as well as by the rejection of the conclusions of a large part of the international Catholic theological community.

Likewise, we take exception to some of the
specific ethical conclusions contained in the encyclical. They are based on an inadequate concept
of natural law: the multiple forms of natural law
theory are ignored, and the fact that competent
philosophers come to different conclusions on this
very question is disregarded.

Even the minority report of the papal commission noted grave difficulty in attempting to present conclusive proof of the immorality of artificial contraception based on natural law. Other defects include: overemphasis on the biological aspects of conjugal relations as ethically normative; undue stress on sexual acts and on the faculty of sex viewed in itself apart from the person and the couple; a static world view which downplays the historical and evolutionary character of humanity in its finite existence, as described in Vatican II's Pastoral Constitution on the Church in the Modern World; unfounded assumptions about the evil consequences of methods of artificial birth control; indifference to Vatican II's assertion that prolonged sexual abstinence may cause faithfulness to be imperiled and its duality of fruitfulness to be ruined; an almost total disregard for the dignity of millions of human beings brought into the world without the slightest possibility of being fed and educated decently.

In actual fact, the encyclical demonstrates no development over the teaching of Pius XI's *Casti Connubii,* whose conclusions have been called into question for grave and serious reasons. These reasons, given a muffled voice at Vatican II, have not been adequately handled by the mere repetition of past teaching.

It is common teaching in the Church that Catholics may dissent from authoritative, non-infallible teachings of the Magisterium, when sufficient reasons for doing so exist.

Therefore, as Roman Catholic theologians, conscious of our duty and our limitations, we conclude that spouses may responsibly decide according to their conscience that artificial contraception in some circumstances is permissible and indeed necessary to preserve and foster the values and sacredness of marriage.

It is our conviction also that true commitment to the mystery of Christ and the Church requires a candid statement of mind at this time by all Catholic theologians.[43]

This is an absolutely unique document. It is safe to say that if a fledgling in theology got this sort of feedback on his examination paper, he would turn to some other endeavor. According to the professors, the Pope had flunked theology.

And yet, despite its haste and olympian condescension, this statement makes clear that the actual content of *Humanae Vitae* was of secondary importance to the signers of the statement. Their true target was the papacy; the real burden of their remarks had to do with the locus of authority in the Church, indeed with the very nature of the Church.

⸗

The Central Issue: What Is the Church?

In reacting as they did to *Humanae Vitae*, the dissenting theologians assumed a novel view of the teaching role of the Church: the function of the Pope is to promulgate and endorse the consensus of believers. This consensus is to be found, the theologians suggest, in the majority report of the papal commission, the special witness of many Catholic couples, the witness of the separated Christian churches, and the international Catholic theological community.

The Pope, of course, acted on another view of the Church, which says that the authority of the Pope does not come, as the dissenting theologians suggest, from the consensus of the faithful, nor even in a more restricted understanding, from the consensus of the bishops. On the contrary, authority flows from the Pope to the bishops and then, in some cases, to the faithful. This is the view of the Church found in *Lumen Gentium*, Vatican II's Dogmatic Constitution on the Church, a document that also derives its authority from the fact that it was promulgated by the Pope:

> The college or body of bishops has for all that no authority unless united with the Roman Pontiff, Peter's successor, as its head, whose primatial authority, let it be added, over all, whether pastors or faithful, remains in its integrity. For the Roman Pontiff, by reason of his office as the Vicar of Christ, namely, and as pastor of the entire Church, has full, supreme, and universal power over the whole Church, a power which he can always exercise unhindered.[44]

In light of this clearly stated ecclesiology in the documents of Vatican II, it seems impetuous of dissenting theologians to question the Pope's ecclesiology and to cite Vatican II as justification for their dissent.

Of course, they might want to balance the above passage with others taken from the acts of that council, and there would be the makings of an interesting theological discussion. But of what interest could such a professional debate be to the faithful?

During the turmoil that followed the appearance of the new encyclical, it is doubtful that Catholics in large numbers hurried to consult the documents of the Second Vatican Council so that they could determine whose ecclesiology was right: the Pope's or that of the dissenting theologians. It is equally doubtful, of course, that many read the statement of the dissenting theologians. And, let's say it, it is unlikely that many Catholics even read *Humanae Vitae* itself.

As the story unfolded, what most were aware of was that the Pope had reaffirmed the Church's ban on birth control and that a growing number of Catholic theologians were contesting his right to do so. Niceties apart, these theologians claimed that one could be as Catholic as the Pope — indeed, they were saying one could be *more* Catholic than the Pope — in refusing to follow the Pope. They created the impression that a rejection of the supreme teaching authority of the Roman Catholic

Church does not logically entail that one should leave the Church. Indeed, they attempted to redefine the nature of the Church in such a way that it was the Pope who was out of step.

These dissenting theologians appealed to the consensus of the members of the Church, but of course, the great majority of laymen and even many priests were caught between conflicting claims to authority. They were being asked to choose between two incompatible ecclesiologies and to answer the following fundamental questions: Is the Church simply the sum of Her members? Is the totality of believers the source of the Church's doctrine? Is the Catholic Faith simply what the majority of Catholics believe, such that the role of the bishops and the Pope is to endorse and express this consensus? Or is Catholic doctrine taught chiefly by the bishops in union with the Pope so that the practice and opinions of many, even conceivably most, Catholics could be in conflict with that doctrine?

It would be bizarre to suggest that a quorum of the people of God had thought through the matter and arrived at the ecclesiology espoused by the signers of the Curran statement. It is especially doubtful that they shared the vision of the magisterial role of theologians set down in that statement.

These dissenting theologians urged the laity to follow their consciences. But unless that advice meant that they should simply do as they pleased, laymen now were faced with a crisis of conscience quite different from the one envisaged by the theologians.

These theologians clearly assumed that they were expressing the common consensus of Catholics to whom the Pope's voice arrived as alien and importunate. In actual fact, of course, what Catholics in the pews heard was a cacophony of conflicting voices, and the severest problem of conscience they had to face was the choice of which voice to attend.

∽

Most Bishops Side with the Pope in 1968
Soon the bishops of the United States weighed in on the side of the Pope. Their statement was made public on July 31 by Archbishop John F. Deardon of Detroit, president of the National Conference of Catholic Bishops:

The sacredness of Christian marriage makes it a special concern of the Church. Its dignity must be carefully safeguarded and its responsibility fulfilled. The recent encyclical letter of Pope Paul VI reflects this concern.

The Holy Father, speaking as the supreme teacher of the Church, has reaffirmed the principles to be followed in forming the Christian conscience of married persons in carrying out their responsibilities.

Recognizing his unique role in the Universal Church, we, the bishops of the Church in the United States, unite with him in calling upon our priests and people to receive with sincerity what he has taught, to study it carefully and form their consciences in its light.

We are aware of the difficulties this teaching lays upon so many of our conscientious married people, but we must face the reality that struggling to live out the word of God will often entail sacrifice.

In confident trust in the firmness of their faith, in their loyalty to the Holy Father and to his office, and in their reliance on divine help, we ask of them a true Christian response to this teaching.[45]

Quite obviously an electric situation was shaping up. The bishops of the United States took quite a different view of the matter than did the dissenting theologians who had signed the draft statement. And yet, strangely enough, several dissenters professed to find in the bishops' statement support for their own protest.

Because of this, Bishop Joseph Bernardin, general secretary of the National Conference of Catholic Bishops, sought to clarify the matter. Bishop Bernardin, asserting that the intent of the bishops' statement was clear, added that the bishops "in no way intend to imply that there is any divergence between their statement and the teaching of the Holy Father. It is true that people must form their conscience, but it is equally true that they have a responsibility to form a correct conscience."[46]

Bishop Bernardin went on to refer to the following passage from *Lumen Gentium:*

Bishops who teach in communion with the Roman Pontiff are to be revered by all as witnesses of divine and Catholic truth; the faithful, for their part, are obliged to submit to their bishops' decision, made in the name of Christ, in matters of Faith and morals, and to adhere to it with a ready and respectful allegiance of mind. This loyal submission of the will and intellect must be given in a special way to the authentic teaching authority of the Roman Pontiff, even when he does not speak *ex cathedra*, in such wise, indeed, that his supreme teaching authority be acknowledged with respect, and that one sincerely adhere to the decisions made by him, conformably with his manifest mind and intention, which is made known principally either by the character of the documents in question, or by the frequency with which a certain doctrine is proposed, or by the manner in which the doctrine is formulated.[47]

On Sunday, August 4, in messages read in each parish, most bishops added their own individual statements of agreement with and loyalty to the Pope. It had been predicted that informed Catholics would ignore *Humanae Vitae*; these strong pro-Vatican statements from most bishops rendered this unlikely. Nowhere would the average Catholic find support for the teaching role the dissenting theologians had arrogated to themselves, a role that apparently bypassed the Pope and the hierarchy.

Whose Church Is It, Anyway?

❦

Laymen Remain Caught in the Middle

Of course, there remained the possibility that many
Catholic couples, informed and uninformed, would find
themselves unable to accept in practice the Church's
stand. No doubt this was true, as it always had been.
The Pope had envisaged such an inability in the encyclical and John Cardinal Heenan of Westminster had urged
the faithful who failed to abide by the ban not to despair,
to continue to frequent the sacraments, and to pray for
the strength to do the right thing.[48] It is always difficult
to do the right thing, particularly in sexual matters, but
the Pope's call for understanding and mercy was something new.

Moral weakness is one thing. The dissenting theologians were defiant on a higher level. They were contesting the very rule of right conduct in the area of marital
relations. They professed to envisage situations in which
a married couple would be obliged in conscience to employ means that the Pope and bishops taught were, of
themselves, morally forbidden. And the theologians did
not speak as if this would be a rare and infrequent case;
they spoke as if it were the rule.

Clearly a crisis was taking shape. Many theologians and priests were separating themselves from a clear consensus among those in whom the teaching office of the Church resides. In doing so, they were invoking against the hierarchy what they took to be a majority of the laity. They were assuring the laity that they could continue to employ artificial means of contraception, that they might even be *obliged* to do so, but that, at any rate, the decision was up to them.

Consider the plight of the faithful in this situation. Despite the alacrity with which some laymen have, without training or authority, assumed the title of theologian, few Catholics would consider themselves in a position to adjudicate the differences between the substance of *Humanae Vitae* and that of the theologians' statements. The latter tended to flatter the laity by appealing to them as informed, educated, mature, and so forth.

But it was clearly an intolerable situation when the simple faithful were forced to choose between the Pope and the bishops, on the one hand, and on the other, theologians and journalists who told them to ignore the Pope and bishops. Fr. Norris Clarke, S.J., professor of philosophy at Fordham University and president of the

American Catholic Philosophical Association, commented that such overt dissent after an encyclical was unique in the history of the Church.

No wonder many asked, "How long can this go on?"

∞

The Chorus of Dissent Grows Louder

But there were soon to be other dissenting voices. At Milwaukee's Marquette University, Fr. Bernard Cooke, together with thirteen members of the theology department, issued a statement. In it, they admitted that the Pope's encyclical was authoritative on the immorality of artificial contraception and must be seriously considered by Catholics. However, they said, *Humanae Vitae* does not preclude their right to "form responsibly their own conscience on the question."[49]

As Msgr. Lambruschini had done, this group made the point that the encyclical was "authentic" but not "infallible." In the opinion of the Marquette group, however, the situation of practical doubt about the immorality of artificial contraception still existed because the Pope had not addressed the points raised against the older doctrine. In their words, "Since Catholic theology has always taught that a grave obligation may never be imposed on

the Christian conscience unless the obligation itself
is absolutely certain, the Pope's encyclical has not
decisively altered the situation of practical doubt." The
encyclical certainly "introduces an important new ele-
ment — his [the Pope's] authoritative judgment on the
issues involved." Nevertheless, we are really in the same
position we were in before the encyclical came out. "Nor
may confessors, preachers, or teachers legitimately go
beyond the Pope and attempt to impose an obligation
which his own encyclical of its own nature cannot
impose."[50]

Again a group of theologians must have seemed to the
average Catholic to be setting themselves in opposition
to the Pope and bishops. They even issued instructions to
confessors and preachers at variance with those given
by the bishops.

While not discussing matters of ecclesiology, the
Marquette group, like those who had signed the Curran
statement, had a view of the teaching authority of theologians that seemed to make it independent of the papal
and episcopal offices. The non-expert could surely be for-
given if he were confused by the advice of the Marquette
group. In what would a "serious consideration" of *Humanae*

Vitae consist if the encyclical amounted to as little as these men said? Moreover, they left little doubt as to what they thought the outcome of that serious consideration would be.

The most outspoken statement of all was issued by Msgr. George Schlichte, rector of Pope John XXIII Seminary, in Weston, Massachusetts. The rector, joined by seven members of the seminary faculty, rejected *Humanae Vitae*, which they found "most disappointing at a time when Roman Catholics are experiencing a new sense of Christian maturity."[51]

They went on to espouse in explicit fashion the ecclesiology that had been given a muffled voice in the Curran statement:

> The Holy Spirit is present first of all in the community of God's people, and those who fail to reflect the consensus of this community damage the effectiveness of the Church's mission. The pronouncement is an expression of a minority view which is contrary to the consensus of the international lay congress in Rome, against the almost unanimous opinion of theologians, and at variance

with the majority report of the papal commission on birth control. This may seem to be a humiliating experience for the entire Roman Catholic Church, but out of it can emerge a more authentic mode of leadership, more sensitive to the spirit of God, and more dedicated to responsible Christian formation.[52]

Once more the Pope had flunked theology. Besides, he was humiliating the Church and damaging the effectiveness of the Church's mission.

∽

"A Catholic Is a Papist"

Now, this is pretty heady stuff. The atmosphere was getting charged. Dr. Samuel Johnson's remark about the Irish has always been applicable to theologians: "They are an honest people; they never speak well of one another." But it is slightly unusual, even for theologians, to say that the Pope, in a solemn document and one in which, after all, he was in agreement with his predecessors and the entire Catholic Tradition on the matter, was impeding the mission of the Church. One expected charges of heresy to start flying, and, sure enough, they soon did.

Borrowing a phrase from the political arena, *America*, the Jesuit weekly, had already warned against making *Humanae Vitae* a "loyalty test." Its editors claimed that the most serious question raised by the new encyclical was not artificial contraception, but the exercise of the teaching authority of the Church. "For our part, we have no doubt that tradition fully vindicates the right of the Pope and bishops to speak on family life and conjugal love. Indeed it does much more than that: it establishes the duty of all Catholics to listen."[53]

In a debate sponsored by the Washington Lay Association, the question quickly became whether Catholics, having listened, were permitted to disagree. In the debate, *Triumph* magazine editor L. Brent Bozell maintained that any Catholic who does not accept the encyclical denies the Pope, denies the Church, and denies Christ, because he is not so much denying truth as authority. Catholics have an obligation to assent. He said that those who call themselves theologians but don't accept the encyclical should not consider themselves capable of serious theological discussion.

In reply, Bozell's opponent, a Jesuit priest, said that he knew of no theological manual, old or new, that would assert that when the Pope speaks fallibly, Catholics must give interior assent when they have serious reasons not to do so.

As his later statement made clear, Bozell had stern advice for such priests:

> Those priests who refuse to accept and faithfully carry out in their pastoral capacity Pope Paul's encyclical on birth control, should leave the Church. Any person who refuses submission to an authoritative teaching by the supreme pontiff on Faith and morals is a schismatic; and simple honesty, greatly honored in the present age, requires him to acknowledge the state of schism.
>
> Any priest whose reason is not persuaded by the Pope's teaching should pray fervently to be among those whom Christ praised because they "have not seen, and yet have believed" (John 20:29). If they will not do this, they should cease pretending to represent the Catholic Church. Otherwise, they will be personally responsible for widening the schism and increasing the scandal.[54]

These are harsh words. But Bozell was not alone. Fellow *Triumph* editor Michael Lawrence was equally severe in the Washington debate. Lawrence said that those who do not accept the right of the Church to teach on moral questions are simply not Roman Catholics. Further, those who say that *Humanae Vitae* should be taken seriously, but who would balance the Pope's teaching with their own private conscience, have a "Protestant view" of conscience. "A Catholic does not have a free conscience."[55]

In other words, while anyone is, of course, free to be a Catholic or not, he is not free as a Catholic to reject what the Church teaches. To do so is to cease to be a Catholic.

Germain Grisez, professor of philosophy at Georgetown University and author of the book *Contraception and the Natural Law*, explained it this way:

The thing that is peculiar to Catholics is that we are papists. I think that the decision is undoubtedly a very hard one, and many people will have to decide whether they want to be papists, that is, Catholic, or not. If one is a Catholic, one is a papist. And if one is a papist, then one cannot say, "Rome has spoken, but the cause goes on." One has to say, "Rome has spoken; the cause is finished."[56]

Chapter Four

Theologians
Whipsaw the Laity

The dissenting theologians did not want to accept so simple an opposition. At least some were quite clear in recognizing the teaching authority of the Pope, but they disagreed about the weight of particular vehicles of that teaching authority, and in particular about the force of the admittedly non-infallible encyclical *Humanae Vitae*.

They held that, although a Catholic had to take it seriously into account, it did not demand unqualified assent. In other words, the encyclical simply was not, as such, the last word on the matter. Catholic couples had to form their own consciences. Thus said the more sophisticated of the dissenting theologians.

Now, what should be made of a dissenting theologian's claim that, although the "official Church" (the Magisterium) teaches one thing (e.g., that contraception, homosexual activity, and other deeds are wrong), there are theologians like him who do not agree and that we must follow our conscience in deciding what we will do in each case? This advice can be understood in several ways.

The dissenting theologian may have a conception of conscience according to which, if you follow your conscience, you are doing the right thing. Thus, if *your* conscience tells you that it is all right to practice contraception, engage in homosexual activity, or perform other forbidden deeds, it is all right *for you* to do so. If *mine* tells me it is not all right, then it would be wrong *for me* to do so. Since our conclusions are opposed, it would seem that one of us is right and the other wrong. We can both be right only if following conscience, whatever it tells you, is always right. And if different consciences hold contradictory judgments, on this view such judgments must be true for the one having them, without any public import.

The Catholic teaching is different: it says that, while each person is obliged to follow his conscience, a person with a wrongly formed conscience may, in following his conscience, perform an evil deed. In such a case, he is responsible for not having properly formed his conscience. As a Catholic, he can have a badly formed conscience only by ignoring the clear and reiterated teaching of the Magisterium.

"But," he might object, "a theologian told me I could ignore the Magisterium." That, of course, does not relieve him of moral responsibility for his evil deed. In order to follow the advice of such a theologian, a Catholic has to assume that the evil deed is somehow morally licit. But the Magisterium tells him it is not.

Therefore, in following his own conscience, he is accepting the judgment of the theologian and rejecting that of the Church. The theologian is urging the faithful to choose what the Church has declared to be morally evil.

Here is the crux of the matter: it is unreasonable to demand that each and every Catholic settle this disagreement for himself. In order to do so, he would have to become a professional philosopher and a professional theologian. Those who accept the advice of dissenting theologians are very unlikely to understand many, if not all, of the arguments they offer on complicated issues such as artificial contraception, homosexual activity, or the ordination of women. Dissenting laymen finally just have to take the dissenting theologians' word that the Church's arguments are flawed.

Now, in contradiction to such dissenters, I say that the Church's arguments in Her pronouncements are both cogent and good. Does this mean that the layman is in the position of accepting either my claim that the Church's arguments are good or the dissenting theologians' claim that they are not? If that were the situation, non-theologians would be in an unenviable position indeed. That fact, however, did not keep dissenting theologians from putting Catholics in such a bind.

∞

Dissenting Theologians Misconstrue the Issue

Prominent Jesuit theologian John G. Milhaven spoke at the annual theological meeting at Woodstock College, whose theme that year was "The Church, American Style." First, he enunciated a general principle: "A Catholic husband and wife have a responsibility to be docile to the Holy Father and obey him. But they also have a responsibility to each other and their children.[57] In other words, *Humanae Vitae* posed for them a significant moral problem that involved a conflict of obligations. On the one hand was the Catholic's duty to attend respectfully to what the Pope and bishops had to say, to obey them; on the other hand was the duty to spouse and children.

Astute readers will have identified the error here already. The dissenting theologians had in fact created for Catholic couples and for Catholics in general quite a different conflict from the one Fr. Milhaven mentioned, and one that is much easier to resolve.

The Pope wrote that artificial contraception is never a licit means of securing the good of the children or the ends of marriage; Fr. Milhaven, on the other hand, asserted that artificial contraception could sometimes be a legitimate means of securing the good of children and the ends of marriage. Indeed, said Fr. Milhaven, Catholic couples might sometimes even be *obliged* to employ the contraceptive means that the Pope had declared morally wrong: "For example, a married couple who have had three children within four years and whose present income and nerves and love just about suffice to make a good, happy family of the five of them — such a couple could well be justified, despite the encyclical, to use contraceptives. In fact, they might even be obliged to."[58]

Fr. Milhaven gave this example as if he were reporting on a moral decision of a conscientious married couple. But, of course, in constructing the case, he was actually offering advice to married couples about moral decisions they might make in the future. He was providing them an allegedly professional and authoritative opinion and one that, as he knew, was in conflict with the one they would be given if they ever got around to reading *Humanae Vitae*. He even upped the ante by suggesting that they might be *obliged* to take the path he was blazing.

And here we reach the very core of the dispute between the dissenting theologians and the Pope — a dispute that most people misconstrued then and misconstrue even now. Fr. Milhaven may have felt he was appealing to the reasoned judgment of married couples, but what he was actually doing was giving them advice that they would accept, not because of the force or subtlety of his reasoning, which was most likely beyond them, but because of his credentials as a priest and as a professional theologian — indeed, as a professor of pastoral theology at Woodstock College.

Fr. Milhaven, then, was not pointing out a conflict between papal authority and Catholic consciences; he was creating a conflict between authorities: the authority of the Pope and the bishops — the Magisterium — on the one hand, and the authority of himself, a Jesuit theologian, on the other.

∞

Dissenting Theologians Cast the Laity Adrift

Some profess to find this conflict a cheering situation; they say that it can only lead to greater moral maturity on the part of Catholics. Now the faithful must make up their own minds and not act because someone has said that such-and-such is the way to act, even if that someone is the Pope. Others ask whether a Catholic's private decision is the measure of the Catholic Faith or whether the Catholic Faith is the measure of a Catholic's private decision.

Fr. Milhaven's defenders might argue that couples should attend to his message regardless of his credentials as a priest and theologian, and that they should focus on his arguments that contraception may be licit and even obligatory for married couples in contrast to the Pope's arguments that it is immoral. Fr. Milhaven gave as the reason for his opinion that unless, in certain circumstances, couples employ contraceptive devices, the ends of marriage will be jeopardized. The Pope had written that the employment of contraceptives already contradicts the very nature of marriage. Fr. Milhaven replied that the Pope was not speaking infallibly. We can assume that Fr. Milhaven was not speaking infallibly either.

So where does that leave the average Catholic couple? Are they expected to be capable of deciding between these opposing views on their intrinsic merits, let alone on their theological weight?

The vast majority of Catholics have to rely on the credibility of those who give them advice. They have to choose between authorities, not between arguments. The dissenting theologians seem almost heedlessly unaware of the anguish that this causes the faithful and the confusion that dissent introduces. To a man, they seem to feel they are alleviating anguish already felt, but they must see that what they have done is to ask the faithful to accept the word of the dissenters and turn a deaf ear to the word of the Pope and the bishops. For laymen, it is not contraception but authority that is the issue: to whom should laymen turn? To the Pope or to dissenting theologians?

❦

Why Theologians Must Defer to the Magisterium
What has been extraordinary about the past thirty years
is that theological discourse seems to have moved from
the seminar room to the pages of the *New York Times*.
Theologians, singly and in groups, have presumed to
urge on Catholics practices in manifest conflict with the
Magisterium. As we have seen from Vatican II itself, this
is not, has never been, and never could be a legitimate
thing for theologians or anyone else in the Church to
do. There is absolutely no justification for theologians'
taking to the streets and seeking to mobilize the faithful
against the Magisterium.

Theologians who object to playing an ecclesial role
subservient to the Magisterium have often said that such
a role would reduce them to the status of parrots who
would merely repeat what the Pope has said. This is an
extraordinary description of the work of the great theologians who have adorned the history of the Church. At
the same time, to suggest that the theologian's task is to
pass judgment on the Magisterium or to propose things
manifestly contrary to it is a description that has no warrant at all.

Now, it is true that things are taught with varying degrees of gravity by the Church. Some teachings are solemnly defined dogmas; most are part of the ordinary Magisterium. Both of these are infallible when they bear on Faith and morals. And in all cases the teaching authority of the Church is itself regulated by Revelation. Indeed, when the Holy Father favors such things as a world court operated by the United Nations, Catholics recognize this as merely his opinion. It is not a matter of Faith and morals, and it has never before been advocated. To disagree with the Pope on this is surely permissible.

But when the Magisterium bears on its proper object of Faith and morals and when, as in the matter of the nature of marriage and the marital act and the sinfulness of contraception, the Magisterium has spoken repeatedly, consistently, and clearly for generations, all the conditions for infallibility as they are laid down in *Lumen Gentium* seem to be met, which means that Catholics — theologians included — must assent to these teachings.

∽

How Theologians Should Operate

But suppose someone could show that such teachings were not infallible. What would follow from that?

If *Humanae Vitae*, or any other serious teaching, were a reformable, non-infallible doctrine, theologians who thought that they saw flaws in the scriptural or traditional basis for the teaching and who thought that the reasoning behind the teaching was open to criticism would, of course, develop their thoughts. They would show how the arguments in *Humanae Vitae* fail to make their case. They would discuss this with other theologians. Exchanges in the theological journals would take place. Other theologians would respond. A protracted exchange would go on. The case against the teaching and the case for it would be argued and reargued.

Imagine that those who thought that the reformable doctrine ought to be reformed prevailed. Would that serve to remove the teaching from the books? No, the reformers would have to present their arguments to the Pope and bishops, who would then act on the matter.

Discussions of the pros and cons of a magisterial teaching is the proper function of theologians. At various times, great theologians have raised difficulties with the doctrine of the Trinity, the Incarnation, and every item in the Creed. St. Thomas Aquinas's *Summa Theologica* is constructed on the basis of such objections and difficulties.

This is the meat and drink of theology as it is of philosophy. But as Cardinal Newman said, "Ten thousand difficulties do not make a doubt":[59] the theologian is not engaged in a skeptical undertaking. As he subjects Revelation to scrutiny, he is working to deepen his own faith and helping us to deepen ours.

Who is the addressee of such theological discourse? Primarily other theologians. In order to follow what the theologian is saying, more is required than faith and reason. There are many things we would have to learn in order to appreciate fully what is going on in most theological discussions. St. Ambrose said that Christ did not become man in order that man might become a theologian. That means among other things that one need not be a theologian in order to be a Christian, or a saint.

The task of the theologian is one that relates to the whole Church: his is an ecclesial role. And as such it is necessarily related to the Magisterium. As we have seen from the document *Lumen Gentium*, theologians do not constitute another and competing Magisterium. Nothing said by a theologian, as such, is binding on any other Catholic. Nothing said by a group — even a large group — of theologians is, as such, binding on other Catholics.

This means that if, in the case of contraception, the ordination of women, or any other controverted teaching, we learned that it was a reformable doctrine, and we knew that theologians were discussing it, and we discovered further that many of them had concluded that the doctrine could be reformed, their conclusion would nonetheless have no binding power on the Church. Rather, they would submit their thoughts to the Magisterium and would await its decision in obedience.

All of this would be appropriate, fitting, and perfectly ordinary.

∽

Faithful Theologians Challenge the Dissenters
A central point in the Curran statement, as well as in that of the Marquette group, is that, with respect to a non-infallible statement, a Catholic can withhold assent if he has serious reasons for doing so. Yet there is not even a consensus among theologians about this point. Fr. Charles Meyer, professor of theology at St. Mary of the Lake Seminary in Mundelein, Illinois, at the end of

a calm and good-natured analysis, disagreed sharply with
the Curran statement:

> As their major premise, they place the proposition
> that it is the common teaching of the Church that
> Catholics may dissent from authoritative but
> non-infallible teachings of the Magisterium when
> sufficient reasons for doing so exist. This is, *salva
> reverentia,* not quite true. Common teaching holds
> that those who are *experts* in the field may with-
> hold their assent while they propose to the proper
> authority reasons which *have not yet been considered*
> by the Magisterium in reaching its decision.
>
> But no common opinion would sanction
> their setting themselves up as an independent
> Magisterium. No opinion would allow them to
> authorize the faithful to follow a course at variance
> with that taken by the only Magisterium the
> Church of Christ knows.
>
> If there is an underlying fallacy in the state-
> ment of the theologians, it is perhaps that truth
> can be attained more readily through a democratic
> process than by an authoritarian decision. Of

course, it is clear that, apart from any invocation
of the charism of infallibility, truth as such cannot
be attained in either way. At most, all that can be
achieved is practical certainty, a certainty that can
be normative for personal decision in acting.

It is difficult to see how, in pursuing this certainty, those who profess their commitment to
the recognition of the Magisterium, those who acknowledge authentic leadership in the Church as a
heritage from Christ, can still remain dedicated to
that principle and that leadership and refuse to follow. Their position is, to say the least, somewhat
anomalous.[60]

If Fr. Meyer is right on this absolutely crucial point in
the stand of the dissenting theologians, "anomalous" may
seem an altogether too mild word for their position. Not
only have they withheld assent; they have also urged others to counsel the faithful that they are under no obligation to follow the teaching of *Humanae Vitae* and other
solemnly defined teachings of the Church.

How much worse than anomalous is the situation of
those who heed their advice.

∽

The Position of Laymen Worsens

Of course, Fr. Meyer's statement puts laymen into an even more difficult position. Now they are not simply being asked to choose between the professed authority of the dissenting theologians, on the one hand, and the Pope and bishops, on the other; they are faced with a fundamental conflict between theologians: the dissenters versus theologians such as Fr. Meyer, who tell us that there is an underlying fallacy in the stand of the dissenters who have been issuing statements and even appearing on television.

How exquisitely mature the faithful will have to be to work their way through this maze! It looks as if laymen are going to need a doctorate in theology in order to have an opinion at all, and that will merely license them to enter an endless dispute.

The Pope, following the initial reactions to *Humanae Vitae*, had this to say:

> Our encyclical *Humanae Vitae* has caused many reactions. But as far as we recall, the Pope has never received so many spontaneous messages of

gratitude and approval for the publication of a document as on this occasion. And these messages have poured in from every part of the world and from every class of people. We mention this to express our cordial thanks to all those who have welcomed our encyclical letter and assured us of their support. May the Lord bless them.

We know, of course, that there are many who have not appreciated our teaching, and not a few have opposed it. We can, in a sense, understand their lack of comprehension and even their opposition. Our decision is not an easy one. It is not in line with a practice unfortunately widespread today which is regarded as convenient and, on the surface, helpful to family harmony and love.

Once again we would remind you that the ruling we have reaffirmed is not our own. It originates from the very structure of life and love and human dignity, and is thus derived from the law of God. It does not ignore the sociological and demographic conditions of our time. Contrary to what some seem to suppose, it is not in itself opposed to the rational limitation of births. It is not opposed to scientific research and therapeutic treatment, and still less to truly responsible parenthood. It does not even conflict with family peace and harmony. It is just a moral law — demanding and austere — which is still binding today. It forbids the use of means which are directed against procreation and which thus degrade the purity of love and the purpose of married life.[61]

The Pope's calm and forbearance toward his critics, while he held firmly to the teaching of *Humanae Vitae*, is a lesson not to be missed. He reveals no inclination to hurl anathemas, to purge or expel. Absent from the encyclical as well as from subsequent papal comments is any exultant or triumphant tone. The tone of the encyclical is one of sadness, almost reluctance, which then gives way to calm confidence before the manifest truth of its message. Paul knows the hardness of his teaching, but he also knows that it is not his but God's.

It is clear that 1968 marked the beginning of dissent in the Church. It would be impossible to find at any earlier time a claim that theologians had the professional task of appraising and assessing magisterial teachings, of accepting or rejecting them. Now it was as if, when the Pope spoke, the theologians first scrutinized what he had said to see whether it was acceptable to them or not. This was utterly new, and it did not begin with Vatican II, but with *Humanae Vitae*.

This is how matters stood in the weeks after *Humanae Vitae* appeared. There is no doubt that the long delay before it appeared — more than two and a half years after the close of the council — and the good-faith assumption of many that the Church's ban could and would be lifted, are mitigating circumstances. Even so, the reaction was unprecedented.

At the time, no one could have known how fateful the heedless dissent from *Humanae Vitae* would be. We are still feeling the effects of it.

It created a crisis of authority in the Church and put the laity in the impossible position of having to adjudicate conflicts between the Magisterium and the insistent voices of dissenting theologians, and even, at times, conflicts between faithful and dissenting theologians. No wonder things declined after 1968.

Chapter Five

The Vatican Finally
Responds to Dissent

In the years after Vatican II, the liberal/conservative polarity that had been established by most reports of the sessions of Vatican II continued to serve as a popular explanation of quarrels among Catholics. There were liberals, and there were conservatives. They had struggled during the council, and the liberals had won. In the liberal view, the drama of the postconciliar period lay in conservative attempts to turn back the clock and undo the work of the council.

As time passed, the Vatican was increasingly portrayed as the enemy of Vatican II; and by the mid-1980s, Joseph Cardinal Ratzinger, Prefect of the Congregation for the Doctrine of the Faith, was the favored target of dissenters. Some even came to see the Holy Father himself, now John Paul II, as the enemy of the council and the foe of reform.

∾

Dissent Had Become Institutionalized

In 1968, *Humanae Vitae* was met with defiance. After that, since it had encountered few obstacles, defiance became the standard theological response to magisterial documents. Dissenting theologians could be counted on to question, criticize, and even dismiss papal encyclicals and statements by Vatican officials. One favorite tactic was simply to predict that a document would be ignored.

The confusion that began in the wake of *Humanae Vitae* came to characterize the Church. On every significant question, there came to be two opposed schools: the liberal and the conservative. The fact that the so-called conservative side was all but identified with the Pope and the bishops posed little problem for those who saw themselves as a counter-Magisterium and had elevated to the level of doctrine the notion that anything short of a solemn infallible pronouncement could be safely challenged.

For twenty years thereafter, dissent was allowed to continue unabated. It became institutionalized. Catholic universities became the usual habitat of dissenting theologians, and many Catholic universities, in Msgr. Kelly's phrase, essentially declared independence from the Catholic Church.[62] They adopted the view that the teaching Church was an alien, off-campus force, and that to permit it to play any role on campus would be to compromise academic freedom. Dissenters were offered sanctuary in theology departments of Catholic universities, where, from tenured posts, they dismissed and even scoffed at magisterial pronouncements, even teaching their students to do so, all without interference from the divinely appointed teachers of the Catholic Church.

These universities trained future teachers, for universities, colleges, and high schools; they trained directors of religious education. For years, students of these dissenting theologians continued to fan out into positions in the Church, taking with them the curious notion that they operated in independence of the Magisterium. They promulgated the doctrines of dissenters, not of the Magisterium.

Thus it was not surprising when Thomas Sheehan wrote in the *New York Review of Books* that dissenters had seized control of the Church in America. With unabashed triumphalism, he crowed that a "liberal consensus" of theologians — that is, anti-papal Catholics — controlled the seminaries, the universities, and other important positions in the Church.[63] Such boasting bothered even his friends, but it was difficult to falsify his claim.

Progressives had won the battle of Vatican II. Progressives had prevailed in the struggles that followed the council. And what is wrong with that? Only that the victory Sheehan described was a victory over the Magisterium. The Pope was being consigned to the ash heap of Church history.

The situation was aggravated by the fact that dissenters controlled the means of communication. It was dissenters whose opinion was sought whenever the Vatican spoke, the secular media knowing they could count on a negative reaction.

If the years from the end of the Second Vatican Council until the publication of *Humanae Vitae* had sowed confusion among the faithful, the twenty years afterward, during which dissent was allowed to become entrenched, all but drowned out the magisterial voice for many Catholics.

◦✤◦

Cardinal Ratzinger Sends a Warning

Finally, in 1985, two events occurred that suggested that the Vatican realized the dimensions of the problem. First, there was *The Ratzinger Report*, a book-length interview with Joseph Cardinal Ratzinger by the brilliant Italian journalist Vittorio Messori. In the interview, Cardinal Ratzinger spoke matter-of-factly and unequivocally of the grave problems that beset the postconciliar Church.

Second, later that year, there was the convening of the Second Extraordinary Synod to commemorate the twentieth anniversary of the close of Vatican II.

Friend and foe alike saw a connection between these two events.

The Ratzinger Report and the Second Extraordinary Synod acknowledged and then examined officially the false spirit of Vatican II. Dissenters saw in both events efforts to roll back history, to repudiate the council, to effect a restoration. The Church, however, in these ways openly acknowledged that efforts had been made in the previous twenty years to use Vatican II for purposes quite alien to the council. In *The Ratzinger Report* and the 1985 synod, the true spirit, as well as the letter, of the council provided the Church a means of showing that it was the self-described progressives — rather than the Pope and the Magisterium — who were out of step with Vatican II.

A dozen years and more have passed since *The Ratzinger Report* and the Second Extraordinary Synod. Reading them now, one is struck by their restraint; it may be difficult to understand why, at the time, they elicited panic from dissenters.

✢

The Patience of the Vatican Is Great

Joseph Cardinal Ratzinger is Prefect of the Congregation for the Doctrine of the Faith — once the Holy Office of the Roman Inquisition, as hostile writers invariably add. He holds the most important office in the Church after the Pope himself. Sometimes called the *Panzer-Kardinal* ("iron-clad cardinal"),[64] he is often accused by dissenters as seeking to dismantle Vatican II.

One of the great mysteries of the post–Vatican II period is why a dissenter would remain in the Church if he thought that the person chiefly responsible for overseeing the purity of the Faith was engaged in dismantling it. But equally mysterious, perhaps, is the long patience that has been shown theologians and others who defiantly and publicly reject the Magisterium, set themselves up as anti-popes who assure the faithful that they need not accept such encyclicals as *Humanae Vitae*, and yet continue in their posts, prospering and being promoted.

By 1985, the confusion of authorities that emerged in the aftermath of Paul VI's most famous encyclical had become institutionalized. On the one hand, there was the Magisterium, the Pope, and the bishops; on the other hand, the theologians who considered themselves a second and rival Magisterium. On the matter of contraception and a host of other issues, the Magisterium spoke; and then the dissenting theologians, with varying degrees of civility, dismissed the Magisterium and told Catholics they could follow their own consciences — that is, follow the advice of the theologians.

In retrospect, it seems incredible that this situation went unaddressed until 1985, but so it was. Not that the Magisterium was silent — far from it. Never had such a flood of encyclicals and other documents come out of Rome. But almost without exception, they received the same treatment as *Humanae Vitae*. Momentary clarity was replaced with the familiar obscurity.

❧

What the Cardinal Said

Where did the Vatican stand in 1985, as evidenced by *The Ratzinger Report* and the synod?

Cardinal Ratzinger began his interview with a ringing defense of Vatican II and a reminder that the Catholic who accepts that council must also and for the same reasons accept Vatican I, the Council of Trent, and all other councils. He rejected the notion that Vatican II represented a breach with the previous history of the Church. Like all councils, he said, Vatican II derives its authority from the Pope and the bishops in union with him: it is as silly to reject Vatican II and appeal to previous councils as it is to profess to embrace Vatican II and dismiss earlier councils.[65]

What went wrong with Vatican II?

Not its teachings, said Cardinal Ratzinger — not the documents that were promulgated, but the false interpretations of them in the postconciliar period. Cardinal Ratzinger noted that it was undeniable that the years since the council had been a bad period for the Catholic Church. After the council, things happened that were "in striking contrast"[66] to the aspirations of John XXIII in

calling it and of Paul VI in continuing it. These popes
and the Fathers of the council had expected a new unity
among Catholics and a missionary zeal; instead there has
been division and dissent. Cardinal Ratzinger cited Paul
VI's remark that in the Church, we seem to have passed
from self-criticism to self-destruction.[67] Much of this
destructive history, the cardinal noted, has been carried
on under the banner of "the spirit of Vatican II," but the
troubles in the Church have not been due to Vatican II
itself.

Their *external* cause has been the cultural revolution
that has shaken the West: the radical liberal ideology
with its individualistic, rationalistic, and hedonist cast.
Their *internal* cause has been the hidden aggressive and
centrifugal forces — sometimes malicious, sometimes
not — that have sought to embrace the worst aspects of
modernity.

Cardinal Ratzinger saw this as part of the "anti-spirit
of Vatican II,"[68] whose roots lay in the assumption that
the history of the Church began with Vatican II as from
square one. Confusion in many areas is the result. Lack
of clarity about the nature of the priesthood has helped
propel many priests into the lay state and even out of the

Faith. National episcopal conferences, in their meetings, seemed to have reduced each bishop to the status of one vote among many, even though each bishop is in fact master of the Faith in his diocese and directly related to the Holy Father. Scripture studies seemed to have been divorced from the Church. Catholics had lost the sense of Original Sin and succumbed to moral permissiveness and confusion about marriage. Liturgical reform had developed in ways wholly unintended and unacceptable, and modern Catholics tended to downplay even Hell and the Devil.

Clearly Cardinal Ratzinger and the Vatican were unhappy with the course the Church had taken since Vatican II. Many think that this dissatisfaction led directly to the Second Extraordinary Synod.

∽

The Vatican Tries to Take Back the Council
On January 25, 1985, speaking in the church called St. Paul Outside-the-Walls, Pope John Paul II announced that an extraordinary synod of bishops would take place in the Vatican, beginning on November 25 and closing on December 8, twenty years to the day after the close of the Second Vatican Council. The announcement

was almost as surprising as John XXIII's calling of the council:

This year is the twentieth anniversary of the conclusion of the Second Vatican Council, whose first
announcement, as we well recall, was made by my
predecessor John XXIII, of venerated memory, in
this very basilica on this same day, the 25th of
January, 1959. Vatican II remains the fundamental
event in the life of the modern Church: fundamental for examining the riches entrusted to Her
by Christ who, in Her and by means of Her, pro-
longs and communicates to man the *mysterium
salutis*, the work of Redemption; fundamental for
fruitful contact with the modern world for the purpose of evangelization and dialogue on all levels
and with people of upright conscience.[69]

The Pope had been a young bishop who participated
in the council; like Paul VI, he had dedicated his papacy
to implementing the teachings of the council. It is the
mark of tradition to keep hearing echoes of the past, the
coming around again of dates to remember, pushing into
the future with those memories sustaining the soul.

Throughout the period between the announcement of the synod and its start, this note of commemoration would be struck again and again. The Holy Father would even use, in a special context, the word "nostalgia." This should be emphasized because, incredibly, in the months before the synod, and even during it, there were those who considered the synod an effort to repeal Vatican II.

Of course there were many who had reason to fear. There was one sense of "Vatican II" that was indeed threatened by this extraordinary synod: the sense embodied in the notion of the anti-spirit of Vatican II that Cardinal Ratzinger had earlier identified as the enemy of the council. There is a saying that there is no position so absurd that some philosopher has not espoused it. So, too, in the twenty years after Vatican II, it seemed that there was no theory or practice so outrageous that some theologian could not be found to say that it followed from the spirit of Vatican II. During those two decades, the council had been used as a weapon by trendy catechists, creative liturgists, and antinomian moral theologians.

Many good souls had suffered much during those twenty years — the postconciliar years. They saw the Church all but disintegrate before their eyes, while voices spoke cheerfully of the progress that was being made, of the new maturity that was evident. The flight from the priesthood and from religious life did not seem like progress to the simple faithful, nor did Liturgies that seemed bent on making the Mass a banal get-together or overtly sacrilegious.

The Second Extraordinary Synod, called to verify, celebrate, and promote Vatican II, could hardly overlook this crisis. *The Ratzinger Report* had distinguished *post concilium* from *propter concilium*: Cardinal Ratzinger argued that not everything that had come after the council and claimed parentage in it was the legitimate offspring of it.

The sessions of the synod were closed to the press, but there were constant briefings in the press office and mimeographed handouts in Latin and various modern languages. It is good to get some sense of how the Church saw Herself twenty years after the close of Vatican II.

∽

What the Bishops Saw

Cardinal Danneels of Brussels had the task of melding together the responses to questions sent out to the bishops prior to the meeting, which would provide an agenda for the sessions. He noted that negative points were made with great frequency and realism.

Many bishops had pointed out that the liturgical renewal had been insufficiently prepared for, with many priests forgetting that the Liturgy is the patrimony of the whole Church, not a personal performance. Emphasis on the Word of God had sometimes isolated the Bible from its living context, Tradition. "This has come about because of a subjectivism that tries to take the place of ecclesial understanding and the authentic interpretation of the Magisterium."[70]

In some countries, he noted, there is a problem of catechesis. "The gravest problem seems to be in the area of the relationship between morals and the Magisterium of the Church."[71]

But an equally serious problem lay in confusion about the very nature of the Church, and the loss of the sense that She is a mystery.

A brief speech in particular, that of Bernard Cardinal Law of Boston, catches the flavor of the synod, both in its endorsement of the Second Vatican Council and in its acknowledgment of the problems that came after it and needed immediate attention:

The unfolding of the council and the joy of beginning a life of priestly ministry coincided in my life,
for I had been recently ordained when the council
began. The blessing of the council recorded as ex-
periences of the Church throughout the world and
related by Cardinal Danneels are blessings to
which I, too, give witness. . . .

The Sacred Deposit of Faith nourished the
Church before, during, and after the council. . . . Vatican Council II restated in an effective way for our
day this core of Faith. Ideas have consequences, and
where there has been an appropriation of the full and
authentic teaching of the council, there have been
the many positive consequences already recorded.

Those twenty years have seen negative consequences as well. Not consequences of the ideas of
Faith which underlie the documents of the council, but consequences rooted in a secularization of
the Church's teaching and mission. . . .

Cause for pastoral anxiety is seen in the lack of
perseverance of religious and priests, the breakdown
in marital fidelity and family life, the dwindling
attendance at the Sunday Eucharistic celebration,

the decline in the recognition of the sacrament of Penance. Concern is caused by theoretical and practical ecclesiologies which do violence to the council's teaching on the Church. . . . All too often, public dissent is exalted to the status of a theological method and is even institutionalized in Catholic faculties and universities. . . .

Studying these phenomena in the light of faith affords us a strong reminder of our call to be *doctores et magistri fidei* ["teachers and guardians of the Faith"]. . . .

I suggest the establishment of a special commission of cardinals to prepare the draft of a conciliar catechism. . . .

Ideas do indeed have consequences, and as *doctores et magistri fidei*, we must clearly teach those ideas expressive of the Sacred Deposit of Faith.[72]

Cardinal Law's speech is quintessentially American, yet profoundly Catholic. The reference to the deposit of Faith evokes John XXIII's announcement of the council, and the notion of bishops as teachers and guardians of the Faith is pitted against the secularization of the

Church's teaching and mission. In his sense of the Church as communion, Cardinal Law picks up a prominent theme in the Final Report of the synod. His call for a conciliar catechism also figures prominently in the Final Report: it was one of three suggestions that the Pope particularly welcomed.

In the press office, there were many journalism veterans of Vatican II. Like old fire horses, they had the smell of smoke in their nostrils once more, and they grumbled about a dismantling of the council. But they were wrong.

∞

What the Synod Decided

The synod was convoked to celebrate, verify, and promote Vatican II. In their Final Report, the bishops agreed that accurate knowledge and application of the council, both its letter and its spirit, were lacking — and were imperative. The Church's very nature had become obscured and had to be made clear again to the faithful. The Church, they pointed out, is a mystery, and they lamented the tendency to see it as just another organization.

> We are probably not immune from all responsibility for the fact that especially the young critically consider the Church a pure institution. Have we

not perhaps favored this opinion in them by speaking too much of the renewal of the Church's external structures and too little of God and of Christ? From time to time there has also been a lack of the discernment of spirits, with the failure to correctly distinguish between a legitimate openness of the council to the world and the acceptance of a secularized world's mentality and order of values.[73]

As for the Church Herself:

The Council has described the Church in diverse ways: as the people of God, the body of Christ, the bride of Christ, the temple of the Holy Spirit, the family of God. These descriptions of the Church complete one another and must be understood in the light of the Mystery of Christ or of the Church in Christ. We cannot replace a false unilateral vision of the Church as purely hierarchical with a new sociological conception which is also unilateral.[74]

What about the doctrinal chaos created by dissenting theologians? Given the state of the Church in 1985, the Final Report makes its point with amazing gentleness:

Theology, according to the well-known description of St. Anselm, is "faith seeking understanding." Since all Christians must account for the hope that is in them (cf. 1 Peter 3:15), theology is specifically necessary to the life of the Church today. With joy we recognize what has been done by theologians to elaborate the documents of Vatican Council II and to help toward their faithful interpretation and fruit-ful application. . . . But on the other hand, we regret that the theological discussions of our day have some-times occasioned confusion among the faithful.[75]

To remedy this confusion caused by theologians, the bishops formally recommended that a catechism or com-pendium of Catholic doctrine be compiled. This eventu-ated in the *Catechism of the Catholic Church,* which, when it appeared in 1992, was predictably attacked and dis-missed by various theologians and theological symposia.

⁂

What the Synod Accomplished

It was the consensus of journalists in the press office that the 1985 synod was a win for conservatives, and there was much speculation about the future. Would those who had suffered for their orthodoxy during the past twenty years be magnanimous now? The Church clearly intended to get the council back, letter and spirit, and go on from there. Would those who had been the cause of much of the confusion now welcome this effort to get things back on the right track? Would bishops truly act as masters and teachers of the Faith in their dioceses? Would steps be taken to counter the worldwide assault by dissenting theologians on the Magisterium, and to undo the consequent disruption and distortion of Catholic moral teaching?

The answer to all these questions, by and large, was no.

It still is. Today it is the rare bishop who is in charge of the bureaucracy that has metastasized around him. Earlier, Thomas Sheehan had boasted that anti-papal Catholics dominated seminary faculties and university departments of theology; now they are often in control of chanceries. Too many bishops are surrounded by bureaucracies that bear the stamp of dissident theology.

To be sure, here and there, one finds a courageous prelate, a good seminary, or a theologian deserving of the name, but in the parishes, all too often there is the mark of the dissenters rather than of the Magisterium.

As the dissenters might have said, "We are legion."[76]

Chapter Six

Dissenting Theologians
Resist Professing
Their Faith

Four years later, in 1989, the Church sought to ensure that those who exercise office or teach in the name of the Church share the Faith of the Church. The Vatican announced that such individuals had to make a profession of Faith and take an oath of fidelity to the teachings of the Church. Of course, this applied to those who taught Catholic theology. It is worth reading both of these documents[77] before we consider how theologians responded to them. The Profession of Faith is as follows:

Profession of Faith

I, N., with firm faith believe and profess everything that is contained in the symbol of faith: namely:

I believe in one God, the Father, the Almighty, maker of Heaven and Earth, of all that is seen and unseen. I believe in one Lord, Jesus Christ, the only Son of God, eternally begotten of the Father, God from God, Light from Light, true God from true God, begotten, not made, one in being with the Father. Through Him all things were made. For us men and for our salvation He came down from Heaven: by the power of the Holy Spirit, He was born of the Virgin Mary, and became man. For our sake He was crucified under Pontius Pilate; He suffered, died, and was buried. On the third day He rose again in fulfillment of the Scriptures; He ascended into Heaven and is seated at the right hand of the Father. He will come again in glory to judge the living and the dead, and His kingdom will have no end. I believe in the Holy Spirit, the Lord, the giver of life, who proceeds from the Father and the Son. With the Father and the Son He is worshiped and glorified. He has spoken through the prophets. I believe in the one, holy, catholic, and apostolic Church. I acknowledge one baptism for the forgiveness of sins. I look for the resurrection of the dead, and the life of the world to come. Amen.

With firm faith I believe as well everything contained in God's word, written or handed down in tradition and proposed by the Church — whether in solemn judgment or in the ordinary and universal Magisterium — as divinely revealed and calling for faith.

I also firmly accept and hold each and every thing that is proposed by that same Church definitively with regard to teaching concerning Faith or morals.

What is more, I adhere with religious submission of will and intellect to the teachings which either the Roman Pontiff or the college of bishops enunciate when they exercise the authentic Magisterium, even if they proclaim those teachings in an act that is not definitive.

And the oath for those who exercise authority in the Church is as follows:

Oath of Fidelity

I, N., on assuming the office (name of office), promise that I shall always preserve communion

with the Catholic Church whether in the words I
speak or in the way I act.

With great care and fidelity I shall carry out the
responsibilities by which I am bound in relation
both to the universal Church and to the particular
Church in which I am called to exercise my ser-
vice according to the requirements of the law.

In carrying out my charge, which is committed
to me in the name of the Church, I shall preserve
the deposit of Faith in its entirety, hand it on faithfully, and make it shine forth. As a result, whatso-
ever teachings are contrary I shall shun.

I shall follow and foster the common discipline
of the whole Church and shall look after the ob-
servance of all ecclesiastical laws, especially those
which are contained in the Code of Canon Law.

With Christian obedience I shall associate my-
self with what is expressed by the holy shepherds
as authentic doctors and teachers of the Faith or
established by them as the Church's rulers. And
I shall faithfully assist diocesan bishops so that
apostolic activity, to be exercised by the mandate
and in the name of the Church, is carried out in

the communion of the same Church. May God
help me in this way and the Holy Gospels of God
which I touch with my hands.

∞

Theologians Protest the Oath

This requirement that Catholic theologians who teach
in the name of the Church confess their Faith and swear
their fidelity to the Church seems reasonable to most
people, but not to many theologians. In 1989, they
seemed incensed at the suggestion that their teaching
has anything to do with the evangelizing work of the
Church; strangely, they seemed to regard themselves as
freelancers who would not tolerate anyone monitoring
what they teach.

When asked to take the oath, American theologians
first appointed a committee to study the matter: the
"Catholic Theological Society of America Committee
on the Profession of Faith and the Oath of Fidelity."

Did that mean that these theologians lacked the fidelity called for by Vatican II?

The "Report of the Catholic Theological Society of
America Committee on the Profession of Faith and the
Oath of Fidelity," issued on April 15, 1990, shows that

such a suspicion is well grounded. This report is as hostile and cleverly legalistic a report as you are likely to find. What particularly alarmed this learned body was the requirement that a profession of Faith and an oath of fidelity should be required of those who teach Catholic theology.

The report of the committee subjects the requirement of a profession of Faith and oath of fidelity to a critical analysis on the assumption that there is something bizarre and illegal about it.

It piously takes as its motto Canon 212, no. 3:

In accord with the knowledge, competence, and preeminence which they possess, the Christian faithful have the right and even at times a duty to manifest to the sacred pastors their opinion on matters which pertain to the good of the Church, and they have a right to make their opinion known to the other Christian faithful, with due regard for the integrity of Faith and morals and reverence toward their pastors, and with consideration for the common good and the dignity of persons.

❧

Theologians Feel Threatened by the Creed
And how did this esteemed body of theologians react
officially to the Church's requirement that they make
a public profession of Faith — that is, profess the
Creed — and swear their fidelity to the Church? The
authors of the report themselves note that the requirement "evoked from many theologians, pastors, and others, responses that range from discouragement and
surprise to outspoken anger and resentment."[78]

These theologians state that such a negative reaction
from many theologians calls for attention and reflection.

Indeed it does, for as you can already see from having
read the Profession of Faith and the Oath of Fidelity, it
is hard to see why any faithful Catholic would have trouble with either one of them. It is as if the military officer
corps refused to be sworn in, or a politician bristled at
being asked to take his oath of office. It is as if the faithful sat sullen and silent at Sunday Mass when asked to
recite the Creed. Have we come to the point at which
the Creed is a menace to theologians?

The report certainly makes it look like a menace to
theologians as they have understood themselves since

1968. By and large out of step with the moral teaching of the Church, they have been trying ever since the appearance of *Humanae Vitae* to justify their opposition to the Magisterium and to Vatican II's strong call to fidelity to the Magisterium.

∞

What the Theologians Said

The Profession of Faith and the Oath of Fidelity threatened the dissenters' claim to be a rival Magisterium. They wanted to continue to be able to ask the faithful to choose between them and the teaching Church.

Of course, the committee report does not propose an outright and simple rejection of what the Holy See requires. As with the earlier dissent about contraception, it gives a deferential nod to the "official" position and then goes on to suggest that there is another, opposed position that is equally Catholic. The writers of the report summarize what they have to say under eight points:

1. The revised Profession of Faith and the new Oath of Fidelity are now part of Church law.

2. All those are bound by it who are mentioned in Canon 833. But fear not: "University teachers of

disciplines which deal with Faith and morals are bound to take them if their positions are under Church control, such as in ecclesiastical faculties and Catholic universities which have been established, are governed, and can be closed by competent ecclesiastical authority. . . ."[79]

Note that this interpretation has the effect of making the requirement inapplicable to theologians in almost all Catholic colleges and universities in America, for very few of them are still owned by the Church or by religious orders in the Church.

3. The history and role of oaths is ambiguous in the Church.

4. There are also serious ambiguities in the text of the Profession of Faith and in the Oath, which suffers from unnuanced generalization.

5. There must accordingly be careful theological and canonical scrutiny of these texts by theologians.

6. Moreover, inclusion of the following passages raises serious problems of a doctrinal, pastoral, and

ecumenical nature: "I also firmly accept and hold each and every thing that is proposed by the same Church definitively with regard to teaching concerning Faith and morals."

What is the problem here? The committee explains: "There are some, for example, who would subsume the teaching on artificial birth control under what is 'definitively proposed.' "[80]

Aha! Here is the source of their discontent. What has defined theologians as a class since 1968 might be threatened by the Oath of Fidelity and the Profession of Faith: theologians taking the oath might have to assent to *Humanae Vitae*, which they had loudly rejected nearly thirty years before.

7. There are no sanctions for not doing what is asked. "It appears appropriate that at this time no action should be taken against those who judge themselves in conscience unable to make this Profession of Faith or take the Oath of Fidelity in the light of the problems surrounding them."[81]

8. All these problems impinge on the question of translating the Latin of the profession and

the oath. The committee notes that "the use of 'dynamic equivalency' in translation provides the possibility of supplying the necessary nuance to insure a correct interpretation. . . ."[82]

It is no accident that the underlying concern of the report is the continuing justification, at least in their own eyes, of rejection of *Humanae Vitae*, and the establishment of themselves as a counter-Magisterium, contrary to the clear teachings of Vatican II.

Such dissent in theology has led to the absence of Catholic orthodoxy from so much of Catholic life today. The revolt of the theologians against *Lumen Gentium* in Vatican II explains more than any other single factor the parlous condition of the Church Herself since Vatican II.

Until theological dissent from clear Church teachings is a thing of the past, the Catholic Church will continue on its current course and the secularization of the Church and our colleges and universities will accelerate. The direct and indirect impact of this on the souls of the faithful at large is incalculable.

In short, what we have now, as evidenced in official statements of theological societies such as this one, is the

institutionalization of the crisis of authority in the
Church. Catholic theologians have declared their independence from the Magisterium and, in the name of a
false understanding of academic freedom, have come to
see the Magisterium as an extrinsic and alien power that
must not be allowed to determine what they teach, even
when they teach in the name of the Church.

∞

The Vatican Threatens to Punish Dissenters
Eight years passed after the appearance of this report of
the Catholic Theological Society of America committee
criticizing the Profession of Faith and the Oath of Fidelity — eight more years of dissent and decline. Now, however, the Magisterium has addressed the dissenters again,
issuing in July 1998 an apostolic letter intended explicitly
to defend the Faith against dissenting theologians. Read
carefully the first sentence of this new apostolic letter,
entitled *Ad Tuendam Fidem* ("To Defend the Faith"):

> To defend the Faith of the Catholic Church against
> errors which arise from some of the faithful, partic-
> ularly from those explicitly engaged in the disci-
> plines of sacred theology, it seems necessary to us,

whose chief task is to confirm our brothers in the
Faith, that to the texts in force in the Code of
Canon Law and in the Canons of the Eastern
Churches there be added norms which expressly
impose the obligation to uphold the truths definitively proposed by the Magisterium of the Church,
making mention of canonical sanctions regarding
the same.[83]

This apostolic letter reads like a response to the committee of the Catholic Theological Society of America.
By writing the obligation of fidelity into canon law itself,
this letter cuts off every avenue of escape for dissenters.
Canon 750 now says:

With divine and Catholic faith is to be believed
everything contained in the word of God, written
and in Tradition, that is to say, in the unique deposit of Faith entrusted to the Church, and proposed as divinely revealed, whether by the solemn
Magisterium of the Church or by Her ordinary and
universal Magisterium, or which is manifested in
the common adherence of the faithful under the
guidance of the sacred Magisterium: all these are

to be held and any teachings contrary to them are to be avoided.

Each and every thing concerning Faith and morals which is definitively taught by the Magisterium of the Church must be firmly embraced and held, that is, whatever is needed to defend and explain the same deposit of Faith in a faithful and holy manner; therefore whoever refuses to accept such definitive propositions is opposed to the teaching of the Catholic Church.[84]

So adamant is the Vatican that dissent can no longer be tolerated that it has written into canon law the prohibition of dissent.

Why has the Vatican taken this forceful step to rein in dissenting theologians? The Profession of Faith and the Oath of Fidelity have become a dead letter; dissenting theologians have excused themselves from taking it, and nothing has changed. Now the Vatican has expanded canon law to forbid dissent and threatens punishment of those who violate the law.

One can only hope and pray that this will finally resolve the crisis that besets the Church today.

Chapter Seven

How to Fix
What Went Wrong
with Vatican II

Since Catholicism is something we receive rather than invent, authority is absolutely essential to it. Who has the divinely given task of preaching, interpreting, and preserving the deposit of Faith? To whom should we turn? Who is the ultimate authority on what Christ asks of us?

Anyone familiar with what Vatican II said about the Church will find this an easy question to answer. The teaching office is invested in the Pope and the bishops of the world in union with him. The Pope is the supreme and universal teacher of Catholics.

Dissenting theologians, however, have told the faithful that, according to Vatican II, they may safely ignore the Pope as moral teacher and may follow their own consciences, formed according to advice the dissenters are giving. In doing this, dissenting theologians have precipitated a crisis. They have whipsawed ordinary Catholics between competing authorities and have done untold damage to the Church.

Since 1968, Catholics have been repeatedly asked to choose between dissenting theologians and the Tradition of the Catholic Church, reaffirmed time and again by the Magisterium, both in Vatican II and since Vatican II in numerous authoritative pronouncements.

That is the choice.

The choice is not between arguments. The choice is between authorities.

∞

Authority Is the Issue

And the choice should be easy to make. Should a Catholic accept the solemn, repeated teaching of the Magisterium and the Pope, who is the Vicar of Christ on earth, or should he accept the assurance of a theologian that he can safely ignore the repeated teaching of the Magisterium and the Pope, the Vicar of Christ on earth?

It is as if someone next to you whispered that you could reject the Sermon on the Mount and still be a good

Christian. It is as if someone said to you that for centuries the Church has been wrong and is still wrong in Her constant teachings: "Trust me. Ignore them, and you'll still be as Catholic as the Pope."

Of course, this is nonsense.

Earlier we saw what Vatican II says about the authority of the Magisterium. The only permissible response of a Catholic to the Church's teaching is to accept it. Not to accept it is to say that you can be a good Catholic while rejecting Christ's Vicar on earth and the Magisterium that was divinely established in order that the deposit of Faith might be transmitted from generation to generation in all its purity.

But what kind of Catholic rejects the solemn teaching of Christ and His Church? It is one thing to fall short of Catholic teaching in our lives, to sin; and it is quite another to reject the measure of action that is proposed by the Church. Too many Catholics have set themselves up as rivals to the Magisterium. The situation is not altered because they do so by taking the word of dissenting theologians that it is all right to do this.

The pattern is clear: What began as a quarrel about sexual morality quickly escalated into a fundamental dispute as to what the Church is and where authority resides when it is a matter of what the Church teaches and what Catholics must believe. We have seen that it is absurd to invoke Vatican II as a warrant for rejecting the Magisterium.

There is simply no justification for refusal to accept the clear teaching of the Pope on matters of Faith and morals. There is no excuse for theologians' telling the faithful to ignore magisterial teachings with which those theologians have difficulties. If the matter of misleading the faithful and deforming consciences were not so serious, the situation would be rendered comical by the fact that the reasons — theological and philosophical — that dissenting theologians offer are so often risibly weak and manifestly defective.

∞

Arguments Are Not the Remedy

Which brings us back to the essential point: You do not need me or anyone else to tell you that the Church's theological arguments work and those of the dissenters do not. The crisis is not about arguments, but about the authority of the Church. Today there is a conflict of authority. Since Vatican II, the Magisterium has spoken

definitively on a host of issues; many Catholics have
rejected these teachings. Some of these Catholics are
wrong; some are right; and they are wrong or right about
what the Church teaches.

This dispute cannot be settled by each Catholic
appraising the arguments on each side. That would be
impossible. For Catholics the question is, "Whose word
should I take? Which authority should I follow?"

When German theologian Karl Rahner licensed his
fellow theologians to dissent publicly from the teaching
of *Humanae Vitae*, he saw this as leading to the possible
reform of its teaching. And the laity? Fr. Rahner cau-
tioned them to avoid scornful criticism and unbridled
insults and to form their consciences.[85]

In order to do this, laymen would have to know the
difference between reformable and non-reformable,
defined statements of doctrine — in short, they would
have to become theologians. More likely, they would just
take his word that the teaching was not infallible.

But the faithful were left with a choice of authorities.
Which authority should they follow? Even a theologian
should know the answer to that: "Lord, to whom should
we go? You alone possess the words of eternal life."[86]

For dissenting theologians to have asserted their dubious authority against that of the Vicar of Christ is a scandal of the first magnitude. It has inflicted deep and lasting wounds on the Church. It has prevented Vatican II from bearing its intended fruit.

∽

Politics Does Not Explain the Council
In light of this fact, let us, in conclusion, review the answer to the question of this book: What went wrong with Vatican II?

Contemporary accounts of Vatican II portrayed it as a battle between two forces, conservative and liberal, the hidebound and progressive. As a result, the documents of the council came to be looked upon as the triumph of one side over the other. The good guys who had won were the progressives.

That such a political division existed among members of the press who covered the council is undeniable. That a similar division could be found among the theological experts who advised individual bishops or national conferences of bishops is also true. And there doubtless were prelates who regarded the members of the Vatican Curia as obstacles to the renewal that John XXIII had called for. Does this mean that the council was a victory for one side and a defeat for the other?

This question indicates the limitations of such a factional interpretation. The Church is not merely a human organization: She is a divinely instituted mystery whose life is guided by the Holy Spirit. Whatever wrangling went on outside St. Peter's, however much a partisan spirit might have been carried within, when the various schemata were argued over and revised, once they received a majority of the votes of the Fathers of the council and were promulgated by Paul VI, they could no longer be looked upon as the product or property of some party within the Church. Now they were regulative of the Faith of all Catholics. No Catholic could presume to reject the council and think that he remained a loyal member of the Church.

∞

Theologians Raise False Expectations

In the years immediately after Vatican II, an exhilaration was felt as the Church went about the implementation of the council. As we have seen, in that halcyon time, it was thought — and not without reason — that the Church's teaching on artificial contraception would change. What many considered a burden on Catholic couples would be lifted. The fear of pregnancy would no longer cause friction and tension; married life would flourish as never before. The commission that was to report to the Pope on the matter arrived at a majority recommending change. Word of this got out. It was taken as the final word. Teaching, pastoral counseling, marriage preparation, and the confessional reflected the anticipated change.

Then on July 29, 1968, Paul VI presented to the world the encyclical *Humanae Vitae*, in which, to the surprise and then the anger of theologians who had staked their professional reputations on a change in the teaching, he eloquently recalled the Catholic conception of marriage and taught that artificial contraception was a denial of the meaning of the marital act and was in itself immoral.

∞

Theologians Call for Disobedience

As we have seen, the reaction of theologians was unprecedented. They publicly took issue with the Pope and pitted their authority against his. This defiance gestured in the direction of the arguments of the encyclical as the bases for their disagreement, but the theologians were really asserting their authority against that of the

Magisterium. They were telling Catholics to ignore the
Pope and listen to them.

How were Catholics to respond to this unprecedented
challenge?

Those who, on the advice — that is, the authority — of dissenting theologians, had begun to practice
contraceptive sex, could be expected to incline toward
the authority of the theologians. But to continue to follow the dissenting theologians now was to join in their
defiance of the Magisterium. Could a Catholic do that?

Yes, they were told. Told by whom? By the dissenting
theologians. Once again, it was a matter of accepting
authority.

The advice was put in terms of following one's conscience: read the encyclical carefully, and then follow
your own conscience. Careful reading apparently meant
that couples were to subject the contents of the encyclical to critical scrutiny and then to accept or reject it. But
what sort of scrutiny was imagined? And is an encyclical
an invitation to that sort of scrutiny, one that might lead
to rejecting it?

Moral theologians would of course — at least at the
beginning of the crisis — want to provide arguments

both for contraception and for their defiance of the Magisterium. That these arguments are all vulnerable to criticism — as they are — is not the present point. The life of Catholics cannot be led on the basis of the outcome of a theological debate, if only because few Catholics are theologians with the competence to assess the various positions.

◌̸

Theologians Provoke a Crisis of Authority
Regardless of the case the moral theologians presented and regardless of their proper task and competence, in 1968, something very different was introduced. In place of the serene and serious intellectual work that theology demands, the Church encountered a mounting insurrection of theologians against the Magisterium. There was no need to take out a full-page ad in the *New York Times* to make a theological point. That was a political act.

In order to justify that political act, a new conception of the Church had to be fashioned, a new notion of where authority lay in the Church and how and by whom it was exercised.

Dissenters claimed that Vatican II justified their defiance of the Magisterium. This was nonsense, of course, but those who were misled by it generally did not go astray on the basis of a careful study of the documents of Vatican II. They accepted the word of the theologians.

This is why, again, it is clear that the crisis in the Church today is not the pitting of one argument against another. The crisis consists in a conflict of authorities. And that crisis has become progressively more complicated. Catholics who took the word of the theologians that they could practice contraception, later had to take their word that they could defy the Magisterium and remain loyal Catholics. Soon they were at ease with their malformed consciences. Their ears grew ever more deaf to the Church's voice as expressed in Vatican II and in so many subsequent pronouncements.

☙

Dissent Has Become a Habit

With time the crisis deepened. At the outset, there had been a conscious and unprecedented dismissal of the Magisterium, something that excited attention and caused dissenters to think of themselves as heroes in a struggle against oppression, something whose revolutionary character was understood. Over the years, dissent became domesticated. A generation of younger theologians was schooled in the notion that their task is somehow distinct from and unguided by the Magisterium.

Today papal documents are routinely subjected to a dismissal that would be impudent if it were not so routine. Defiance is no longer novel. Today it almost seems as if the term "dissenting theologian" should be applied to the few who accept the Magisterium.

But there is an even deeper irony. An endless number of children is no longer the only alternative to contraceptive sex. Natural Family Planning has rendered the alleged basis for dissent against *Humanae Vitae* pointless. Why are dissenting theologians uninterested in or hostile toward Natural Family Planning? Their original concern for a moral way to limit the size of one's family seems to have evaporated now that science has discovered a moral way to do it. Dissent has become merely a habit now and one that has lost its point.

∽

Dissenters Ignore the Vatican's Efforts

The Ratzinger Report called attention to this crisis of authority; the Vatican has attempted to resolve it with efforts such as the 1985 synod, the 1989 Profession of Faith and Oath of Fidelity, the 1992 catechism, and, just recently, the 1998 apostolic letter *Ad Tuendam Fidem,* which makes dissent a violation of canon law and threatens dissenters with punishments. And there has been a flood of other documents and actions intended to reverse the tide of dissent.

None have worked.

✥

How the Crisis Can Be Resolved

It is clear that the solution to the crisis of authority does not lie in arguments alone. Arguments require for their effectiveness that the addressees have ears with which to hear. In any case, the Lord does not generally choose to save His people by means of dialectic. Rather, you and I — and the dissenters — must take a lesson from the wider context in which Pope John Paul II placed his treatment of Christian morality in his encyclical *Veritatis Splendor* ("The Splendor of Truth"). The Pope began with Matthew's account of the rich young man who comes to Jesus, attracted by this Teacher. The young man asks what he must do to be saved. Keep the commandments, our Lord replies. What are the commandments? Jesus reminds the young man, mentioning some of them, and the young man says that he already keeps them. Well then, if he would be perfect, Jesus says, he should sell all he has, give the money to the poor, and follow Jesus.[87]

Here the Pope wants us to see that particular moral questions are specifications of a more general question: What must I do to be saved? Christ founded the Church so that His answer to that question and the grace to receive it could be passed on from generation to generation. He gave to the Holy Father the task of teaching those who desire salvation.

What is needed today is not a refutation of the bad arguments of the dissenters, but a change of heart. *Lumen Gentium*, Vatican II's Dogmatic Constitution on the Church, culminates in a chapter on the Blessed Virgin Mary as Mother of the Church. John XXIII ended his opening address to the council with a prayer to Mary. John Paul II's *Veritatis Splendor*, like so many other writings of the Holy Father, culminates in a prayer to Mary.

At the beginning of these pages, I suggested that it will be by following Mary's wishes as expressed to the children at Fatima that the promise of Vatican II will be fulfilled. She advised prayer and fasting. Prayer and fasting will drive out the demon of dissent and fill the Church once more with the great hope and optimism of Vatican II.

Biographical Note

Born in Minneapolis, Ralph M. McInerny joined
the United States Marines at the age of seventeen. He
went on to graduate from St. Paul Seminary, and earned
a master's degree from the University of Minnesota and a
doctorate from the Pontifical Faculty of Philosophy at
Laval University, Quebec.

Since 1955, Dr. McInerny has taught at Notre Dame
University, where he is the Michael P. Grace Professor
of Medieval Studies and Director of the Jacques Maritain
Center.

Recipient of various awards, as well as the Fulbright
Fellowship and fellowships from the National Endowment for the Arts and the National Endowment for the

Humanities, he is a fellow of the Pontifical Academy of St. Thomas Aquinas and will give the Gifford Lectures at Glasgow in 1999.

Dr. McInerny has written more than sixty books, including numerous novels — among them, his popular Father Dowling mysteries and Andrew Broom mysteries — dozens of works on St. Thomas Aquinas and medieval philosophy, and innumerable articles in academic journals. He is the founder of the journal *Catholic Dossier*, cofounder of *Crisis* magazine, and former editor of *The New Scholasticism*.

Dr. McInerny and his wife, Connie, have been married for more than 45 years, and have six children and fifteen grandchildren.

Endnotes

[1] William Wordsworth, "The French Revolution, as it Appeared to Enthusiasts"; also *The Prelude*, Bk. 9, line 108.

[2] Cf. Ps. 118:24.

[3] *Aeterna Dei Sapientia*, Encyclical commemorating the fifteenth centennial of the death of Pope St. Leo I, November 11, 1961.

[4] Motto of the French Revolution.

[5] Msgr. George A. Kelly, *The Battle for the American Church* (Garden City, New York: Doubleday and Company, Inc., 1979), 59. Msgr. Kelly's list includes Wilfrid and Bernard Ward, Ronald Knox, Maurice Baring, Robert Hugh Benson, Philip Hughes, Gervase and David Matthew, Evelyn Waugh, Sheila Kaye Smith, G. G. Wyndham Lewis, Christopher Dawson, Abbot Vonier, Abbot Butler, Martin D'Arcy, C. C. Martindale, Alfred Noyes, Barbara Ward, Eric Gill, Shane

Leslie, Stephen Dessain, G. K. Chesterton, Hilaire Belloc, E. I. Watkin, Frank Sheed, and Maisie Ward. One could add to the list, of course; Graham Greene and Edith Sitwell come to mind.

[6] Ibid., 60. There Msgr. Kelly discerned François Mauriac, Leon Bloy, Charles Péguy, Jacques Maritain, Étienne Gilson, Reginald Garrigou-Lagrange, Jean Danielou, Henri de Lubac, and Yves Congar. One would hasten to add Paul Claudel, Georges Bernanos, and all those friends of the Maritains mentioned by Raïssa Maritain in her memoirs *We Have Been Friends Together* and *Adventures in Grace*.

[7] Ibid., 61. Msgr. Kelly cites Rudolph Allers, Thomas Vernon Moore, Paul Hanley Furfey, Jerome Kerwin, Waldemar Gurian, Goetz Briefs, Yves Simon, Heinrich Rommen, Stephen Kuttner, John A. Ryan, and John Tracy Ellis.

[8] Evelyn Waugh, "The American Epoch in the Catholic Church," *Life*, September 19, 1949, 140.

[9] Ibid., 155.

[10] Alexis de Tocqueville, *Democracy in America*, Vol. 2, ch. 6.

[11] Kelly, *The Battle for the American Church*, 455.

[12] Ibid., 456.

[13] Ibid., 456-457.

[14] Fr. Antonio Maria Martins, S.J., and Fr. Robert J. Fox, *Documents on Fatima and the Memoirs of Sister Lucia* (Alexandria, South Dakota: Fatima Family Apostolate, 1992), 369.

[15] Floyd Anderson, ed., *Council Daybook: Vatican II, Sessions 1 and 2*, (Washington: National Catholic Welfare Conference, 1965), 25.

[16] Ibid., 26.

[17] Ibid.

[18] Ibid., 29.

[19] Ralph W. Wiltgen, *The Rhine Flows into the Tiber* (New York: Hawthorn Books, Inc., 1967), 28-29.

[20] *Catechism of the Catholic Church*, no. 891.

[21] See Kelly, *The Battle for the American Church*, 411-417.

[22] Philip S. Kaufman, *Why You Can Disagree and Remain a Faithful Catholic* (New York: Crossroad, 1995), 153.

[23] *Lumen Gentium*, no. 22.

[24] *Lumen Gentium*, no. 25.

[25] Ibid.

[26] A 1998 apostolic letter of Pope John Paul II gave force of law to this requirement of Vatican II that theologians be faithful to the Magisterium. Called *Ad Tuendam Fidem*, the letter made deviation from such teachings as Vatican II a violation of canon law subject to punishments up to and including excommunication.

[27] "Cathedral Sit-In," *The Tablet*, August 17, 1968, 829.

[28] "The Argument Goes On," *The Tablet*, August 10, 1968, 796; "Other Reaction to Encyclical," *The Pilot*, August 3, 1968, 8.

[29] "Resigns 'Monsignorship' as Protest to Encyclical," *National Catholic Reporter*, August 21, 1968, 9.

[30] Ibid.

[31] Ibid.

[32] "Crisis in the Church," *The Tablet*, August 3, 1968, 758.

[33] " 'Follow Conscience,' Dr. Küng Says," *The Tablet*, August 17, 1968, 828; " 'Read Pope, Then Follow Conscience,' Küng Says," *National Catholic Reporter*, August 14, 1968, 9.

[34] "World-Wide Reaction Reflects Urgent Concern," *The Pilot*, August 3, 1968, 8.

[35] Thomas D. Roberts, *Contraception and Holiness* (New York: Herder and Herder, 1964).

[36] "Encyclical Binding on Catholics but Is Not Immutable Dogma," *New York Times*, July 30, 1968, 1.

[37] "Bishop Pike Advises 'Speak Out Boldly and Stay In,' " *National Catholic Reporter*, August 14, 1968, 7.

[38] "Press Conference on Encyclical *Humanae Vitae*," *L'Osservatore Romano*, August 8, 1968, 7.

[39] Ibid.

[40] Ibid.

[41] "World-Wide Reaction Reflects Urgent Concern," *The Pilot*, August 3, 1968, 8.

[42] John Leo, "Dissent Is Voiced: Indifference Shown by Many Liberal Catholics in U.S.," *New York Times*, July 30, 1968, 1.

[43] "Text of the Statement by Theologians," *New York Times*, August 31, 1968, 16.

[44] *Lumen Gentium*, no. 22.

[45] "U.S. Bishops Ask Acceptance," *National Catholic Reporter*, August 7, 1968, 4.

[46] Ibid.

[47] *Lumen Gentium*, no. 25 .

[48] "Cardinal Heenan's Pastoral Letter," *The Tablet*, 10 August 1968, 806.

[49] "Reflections on Human Life," special insert to *Our Sunday Visitor*, August 22, 1968.

[50] Ibid.

51 "World-Wide Reaction Reflects Urgent Concern," *The Pilot*, August 3, 1968, 8.

52 Ibid.

53 "An Editorial Statement on 'Human Life,' " *America*, August 17, 1968, 94-95.

54 "Bozell: Some Are in Schism," *National Catholic Reporter*, August 7, 1968, 9.

55 A contemporaneous source was not able to be identified. The accuracy of the quotation was verified by the speaker.

56 "American Theologians Critical," *National Catholic Reporter*, August 7, 1968, 4.

57 "Each Has to Weigh Effects of Disobedience," *National Catholic Reporter*, August 7, 1968, 11.

58 Ibid.

59 John Henry Newman, *Apologia pro Vita Sua*, "Position of My Mind Since 1845."

60 Robert G. Hoyt, ed., *The Birth Control Debate* (Kansas City, Missouri: National Catholic Reporter, 1968), 196-197.

61 "This Is Not Our Ruling — It Is the Law of God," *L'Osservatore Romano*, 8 August 1968, 7.

62 Kelly, *The Battle for the American Church*, 65.

63 Thomas Sheehan, "Revolution in the Church," *New York Review of Books*, June 14, 1984, 35-39.

64 *The Ratzinger Report* (San Francisco: Ignatius Press, 1985), 9.

65 Ibid., 28-29.

66 Ibid., 29.

67 Ibid.

68 Ibid., 34.

[69] "Pope Announces Extraordinary General Assembly of Synod of Bishops to Take Place from 25 November to 8 December," *L'Osservatore Romano*, 4 February 1985, 1.

[70] "Cardinal Danneels: An Overview," *Origins*, December 12, 1985, 428.

[71] Ibid.

[72] Speech given by Bernard Cardinal Law on November 27, 1986. Text provided by the Archdiocese of Boston.

[73] "The Final Report," *Origins*, December 19, 1985, 445.

[74] Ibid., 446-447.

[75] Ibid., 447.

[76] Cf. Luke 8:30.

[77] Endnote Text

[78] Report of the Catholic Theological Society of America Committee on the Profession of Faith and the Oath of Fidelity, April 15, 1990, 1.

[79] Ibid., 115.

[80] Ibid., 79.

[81] Ibid., 116.

[82] Ibid., 117.

[83] This translation of the apostolic letter *Ad Tuendam Fidem* was done by the author, as no official English translation was available at the time this book was written.

[84] *Ad Tuendam Fidem*, nos. 2, 3.

[85] Karl Rahner, "The Encyclical *Humanae Vitae*," *Theological Investigations* (New York: Seabury, 1974), Vol. 11, 284-285.

[86] John 6:68.

[87] Matt. 19:16-21.

Sophia Institute is a nonprofit institution that seeks to restore man's knowledge of eternal truth, including man's knowledge of his own nature, his relation to other persons, and his relation to God.

Sophia Institute Press® serves this end in numerous ways: by publishing translations of foreign works to make them accessible to English-speaking readers; by bringing out-of-print books back into print; and by publishing important new books that fulfill the ideals of Sophia Institute. Sophia Institute Press® makes these high-quality books available to the general public by using advanced technology and by soliciting donations to subsidize its general publishing costs. Your generosity can help Sophia

Institute Press® to provide the public with editions of works containing the enduring wisdom of the ages. Please send your tax-deductible contribution to the address below. We also welcome your questions, comments, and suggestions.

For your free catalog, call:
Toll-free: 1-800-888-9344

or write:
Sophia Institute Press®
Box 5284
Manchester, NH 03108

or visit our website:
www.sophiainstitute.com

Sophia Institute is a tax-exempt institution
as defined by the Internal Revenue Code,
Section 501(c)(3). Tax I.D. 22-2548708.